To: _____

_____

_____

Date: _____

From: _____

_____

_____

# Proverbs Prayers

# Proverbs Prayers

*Praying the Wisdom of Proverbs
into Your Life Every Day*

## JOHN MASON

**Harrison House
Tulsa, Oklahoma**

*Proverbs Prayers*
ISBN 1-57794-390-2
Copyright © 2000 by John Mason
P.O. Box 54996
Tulsa, Oklahoma 74155

Published by Harrison House, Inc.
P.O. Box 35035
Tulsa, Oklahoma 74153

Printed in the United States of America.

# Dedication

It's easy to dedicate this book to the greatest family on earth.

To my wife, Linda, thanks for being my best friend and for laughing with me every day.

To Michelle, for being someone who's given her heart to God.

To Greg, for his peaceful persistence.

To Mike, for his unique creativity.

To Dave, for his boundless energy.

To my parents, Chet and Lorene Mason, for their love, prayers and support.

Prov. 4:7

Wisdom is the principal thing;

therefore get wisdom.

And in all your getting,

get understanding.

# Introduction

Think about it . . . if you could pick one spiritual goal for your life, what would it be? For most people it would include praying and reading their Bible every day, especially the book of Proverbs. Several years ago, when I was reading the Bible, I felt the Lord challenge me to pray what I had just read. When I did, something happened. What I had just read came alive to me. As I did this over time, His Word became clearer and I began to see changes in my life— good changes!

*Proverbs Prayers* is a book written to help you every day. God can change you when you open your life to Him. When you read each proverb and pray the corresponding prayer, you will be asking the Lord to cause every promise and principle from that chapter to come alive in your life. As you do, I believe that God is going to show you some things you've never seen before. You will pray about things that you may have been unaware of or have been avoiding (i.e., anger, lust, your words, etc.) And at the end of thirty-one days, wisdom will be your friend.

Thank you for the privilege of sharing God's Word with you.

Get ready to grow!

# CHAPTER 1

1 The proverbs of Solomon the son of David, king of Israel:
2 To know wisdom and instruction, to perceive the words of understanding,
3 To receive the instruction of wisdom, justice, judgment, and equity;
4 To give prudence to the simple, to the young man knowledge and discretion—
5 A wise man will hear and increase learning, and a man of understanding will attain wise counsel,
6 To understand a proverb and an enigma, the words of the wise and their riddles.
7 The fear of the LORD is the beginning of knowledge, but fools despise wisdom and instruction.
8 My son, hear the instruction of your father, and do not forsake the law of your mother;
9 For they will be a graceful ornament on your head, and chains about your neck.
10 My son, if sinners entice you, do not consent.
11 If they say, "Come with us, let us lie in wait to shed blood; let us lurk secretly for the innocent without cause;
12 Let us swallow them alive like Sheol, and whole, like those who go down to the Pit;
13 We shall find all kinds of precious possessions, we shall fill our houses with spoil;
14 Cast in your lot among us, let us all have one purse"—
15 My son, do not walk in the way with them, keep your foot from their path;
16 For their feet run to evil, and they make haste to shed blood.
17 Surely, in vain the net is spread in the sight of any bird;

18 But they lie in wait for their own blood, they lurk secretly for their own lives.

19 So are the ways of everyone who is greedy for gain; it takes away the life of its owners.

20 Wisdom calls aloud outside; she raises her voice in the open squares.

21 She cries out in the chief concourses, at the openings of the gates in the city she speaks her words:

22 "How long, you simple ones, will you love simplicity? For scorners delight in their scorning, and fools hate knowledge.

23 Turn at my rebuke; surely I will pour out my spirit on you; I will make my words known to you.

24 Because I have called and you refused, I have stretched out my hand and no one regarded,

25 Because you disdained all my counsel, and would have none of my rebuke,

26 I also will laugh at your calamity; I will mock when your terror comes,

27 When your terror comes like a storm, and your destruction comes like a whirlwind, when distress and anguish come upon you.

28 "Then they will call on me, but I will not answer; they will seek me diligently, but they will not find me.

29 Because they hated knowledge and did not choose the fear of the LORD,

30 They would have none of my counsel and despised my every rebuke.

31 Therefore they shall eat the fruit of their own way, and be filled to the full with their own fancies.

32 For the turning away of the simple will slay them, and the complacency of fools will destroy them;

33 But whoever listens to me will dwell safely, and will be secure, without fear of evil."

# CHAPTER 1
## PRAYER

hank You Lord, for Your wisdom in Proverbs. I am forever appreciative of the life-giving instruction and understanding this precious book brings to me. I know You want it to be an indispensable part of my life so I ask You to help me hear Your Words today. As I do, I will increase in learning.

Lead me to receive wise counsel and have a right fear of You in my life. When I do, You entrust supernatural information to me. Help me to avoid being foolish by rejecting Your wisdom and instruction.

Open my eyes to see when sinners cross my path simply to tempt me. If that happens, I choose to immediately take a stand and boldly disagree with them. When they talk persuasively and promise all kinds of success to me, I trust You will stand by me in opposition to them. I don't want to become one of them. Direct my steps and keep me far away from these wrong associations. Keep my feet from heading in the wrong direction.

Lord, are there sinners in my life right now who are trying to persuade me to do the wrong thing? Please show me who they are. I need Your help to keep me free from their influence.

Help me to avoid greed because this kind of selfishness takes away the life that is inside me. Instead, let me conquer greed by becoming a giver.

Is there any area of greed in my life today, Lord? Please show me. Send some opportunities for me to give today.

I ask to be sensitive to hear what wisdom has to say. I don't want to be foolish by hating knowledge. It is my desire to heed Your warning and change through wisdom's reproof. Pour Your Spirit on me and show me Your Words.

Lord, I choose to listen to Your wisdom today. I will not disdain or disregard it. As I do, I trust You will keep me from calamity and terror. Because I fear You and love knowledge, I am confident that You will hear me when I call to You. When I seek You diligently, I will find You. What a privilege it is to follow You and Your wisdom.

Father, help me listen clearly to Your wisdom so I can dwell safely and securely, without fear of evil.

# CHAPTER 2

1 My son, if you receive my words, and treasure my commands within you,

2 So that you incline your ear to wisdom, and apply your heart to understanding;

3 Yes, if you cry out for discernment, and lift up your voice for understanding,

4 If you seek her as silver, and search for her as for hidden treasures;

5 Then you will understand the fear of the LORD, and find the knowledge of God.

6 For the LORD gives wisdom; from His mouth come knowledge and understanding;

7 He stores up sound wisdom for the upright; he is a shield to those who walk uprightly;

8 He guards the paths of justice, and preserves the way of His saints.

9 Then you will understand righteousness and justice, Equity and every good path.

10 When wisdom enters your heart, and knowledge is pleasant to your soul,

11 Discretion will preserve you; understanding will keep you,

12 To deliver you from the way of evil, from the man who speaks perverse things,

13 From those who leave the paths of uprightness to walk in the ways of darkness;

14 Who rejoice in doing evil, and delight in the perversity of the wicked;

15 Whose ways are crooked, and who are devious in their paths;

16 To deliver you from the immoral woman, from the seductress who flatters with her words,

17 Who forsakes the companion of her youth, and forgets the covenant of her God.

18 For her house leads down to death, and her paths to the dead;

19 None who go to her return, nor do they regain the paths of life—

20 So you may walk in the way of goodness, and keep to the paths of righteousness.

21 For the upright will dwell in the land, and the blameless will remain in it;

22 But the wicked will be cut off from the earth, and the unfaithful will be uprooted from it.

# CHAPTER 2
## PRAYER

ord, Your words are so precious to me that I enthusiastically receive them and determine to hide them deep within my heart. Help me to hear Your wisdom and open my heart to understanding. From my innermost being, I yearn for knowledge. I lift up my voice to ask for understanding.

Today, I decide to seek after Your wisdom. I focus my attention and energies to search for it like a person searches for hidden treasure. When I do this, I know You will help me understand how to rightly fear You. What areas are You wanting me to grow more in Your wisdom today?

Lord, I thank You for giving Your wisdom, knowledge and understanding to me today. Show me how to walk with integrity. As I do, I know You are going to protect me. Today, I firmly embrace Your sound wisdom as I do my best to live the righteous life You've called me to live.

Thank You for keeping me on the path of wise judgment today by showing me the right way to go. I am grateful for Your promise of saving me and preserving me as I do what You want me to do. Help me to hear wisdom and let it penetrate deep within my heart. When I do, that knowledge will become pleasant to my soul.

Lord, save me from immoral people, particularly those who have enticing and flattering words. Help me be a person of discretion and understanding because it protects me. Remove any evil person who comes into my life, especially those who speak and say wrong things.

With the help of Your insight and strength, I'm not going to have any relationship with people who don't want to follow You, who choose evil and are happy about it. Thank You for delivering me from them.

Lord, help me walk with good people and stay on the right path today.

# CHAPTER 3

1 My son, do not forget my law, but let your heart keep my commands;

2 For length of days and long life and peace they will add to you.

3 Let not mercy and truth forsake you; bind them around your neck, write them on the tablet of your heart,

4 And so find favor and high esteem in the sight of God and man.

5 Trust in the LORD with all your heart, and lean not on your own understanding;

6 In all your ways acknowledge Him, and He shall direct your paths.

7 Do not be wise in your own eyes; fear the LORD and depart from evil.

8 It will be health to your flesh, and strength to your bones.

9 Honor the LORD with your possessions, and with the first-fruits of all your increase;

10 So your barns will be filled with plenty, and your vats will overflow with new wine.

11 My son, do not despise the chastening of the LORD, nor detest His correction;

12 For whom the LORD loves He corrects, just as a father the son in whom he delights.

13 Happy is the man who finds wisdom, and the man who gains understanding;

14 For her proceeds are better than the profits of silver, and her gain than fine gold.

15 She is more precious than rubies, and all the things you may desire cannot compare with her.

16 Length of days is in her right hand, in her left hand riches and honor.

17 Her ways are ways of pleasantness, and all her paths are peace.

18 She is a tree of life to those who take hold of her, and happy are all who retain her.

19 The LORD by wisdom founded the earth; by understanding He established the heavens;

20 By His knowledge the depths were broken up, and clouds drop down the dew.

21 My son, let them not depart from your eyes—keep sound wisdom and discretion;

22 So they will be life to your soul and grace to your neck.

23 Then you will walk safely in your way, and your foot will not stumble.

24 When you lie down, you will not be afraid; yes, you will lie down and your sleep will be sweet.

25 Do not be afraid of sudden terror, nor of trouble from the wicked when it comes;

26 For the LORD will be your confidence, and will keep your foot from being caught.

27 Do not withhold good from those to whom it is due, when it is in the power of your hand to do so.

28 Do not say to your neighbor, "Go, and come back, and tomorrow I will give it," when you have it with you.

29 Do not devise evil against your neighbor, for he dwells by you for safety's sake.

30 Do not strive with a man without cause, if he has done you no harm.

31 Do not envy the oppressor, and choose none of his ways;

32 For the perverse person is an abomination to the LORD, but His secret counsel is with the upright.

33 The curse of the LORD is on the house of the wicked, but He blesses the home of the just.

34 Surely He scorns the scornful, but gives grace to the humble.

35 The wise shall inherit glory, but shame shall be the legacy of fools.

# CHAPTER 3
## PRAYER

ord, I open my heart again today to obey all Your commandments because they give me a long, peaceful life. I will never forget Your Word. I ask for Your help in letting mercy and truth dominate my life so I can find favor and understanding with You and with others.

Today, I choose to trust You with all of my heart and not depend on my own understanding. Help me to acknowledge You in everything, then I will know exactly which way to go. Lord, I choose to reject the desire of my ego today. I don't want to be wise in my own eyes; so help me to resist pride. Instead, I want to fear You and stay away from evil. When I do, health and strength come into my life.

Today, I choose to honor You with my possessions. I will always give You the firstfruits of any increase that comes into my life. As I do, You bless my life to overflowing.

From this moment on, I'm not going to reject any correction, realignments or adjustments that You bring to me. And Lord, because I am Your child, I won't grow weary of them, even if You have to correct me over and over again because of Your Fatherly love. Is there anything You would like to correct in me today, Lord? Mess with me, Lord. I open my life to Your reorganization.

I thank You today that as I find wisdom and gain understanding, I will be a happier person. Assist me in understanding the value of wisdom and seeing why it is greater than rubies, silver, or fine gold. Your wisdom lengthens my days while bringing marvelous results.

Help me keep wisdom and discretion as an integral part of my life. As I do, Lord, I know that it will bring life to my soul and grace to my life.

When I go to bed at night, keep me from being afraid of anything so I will sleep peacefully. Thank You for delivering me from any unexpected fears of being destroyed. You are my confidence and You will keep me safe.

Lord, I sincerely ask You today to send opportunities for me to do good to others, especially when I can do something to make a genuine difference. Keep me from plotting and cultivating evil against others who have put their trust and confidence in me. Remove envy from my life, especially towards those who are deceitful and greedy. Help me to stay free today from any of these ways.

And thank You, Lord, that my house is not cursed because of wickedness. Your blessing comes on my household as I try to walk justly before You. I pray that I will have a humble attitude today. As I do, I know You will give me grace. I thank You that honor comes to those who walk in Your wisdom.

# CHAPTER 4

1 Hear, my children, the instruction of a father, and give attention to know understanding;

2 For I give you good doctrine: do not forsake my law.

3 When I was my father's son, tender and the only one in the sight of my mother,

4 He also taught me, and said to me: "Let your heart retain my words; keep my commands, and live.

5 Get wisdom! Get understanding! Do not forget, nor turn away from the words of my mouth.

6 Do not forsake her, and she will preserve you; love her, and she will keep you.

7 Wisdom is the principal thing; therefore get wisdom. And in all your getting, get understanding.

8 Exalt her, and she will promote you; she will bring you honor, when you embrace her.

9 She will place on your head an ornament of grace; a crown of glory she will deliver to you."

10 Hear, my son, and receive my sayings, and the years of your life will be many.

11 I have taught you in the way of wisdom; I have led you in right paths.

12 When you walk, your steps will not be hindered, and when you run, you will not stumble.

13 Take firm hold of instruction, do not let go; keep her, for she is your life.

14 Do not enter the path of the wicked, and do not walk in the way of evil.

15 Avoid it, do not travel on it; turn away from it and pass on.

16 For they do not sleep unless they have done evil; and their sleep is taken away unless they make someone fall.

17 For they eat the bread of wickedness, and drink the wine of violence.

18 But the path of the just is like the shining sun, that shines ever brighter unto the perfect day.

19 The way of the wicked is like darkness; they do not know what makes them stumble.

20 My son, give attention to my words; incline your ear to my sayings.

21 Do not let them depart from your eyes; keep them in the midst of your heart;

22 For they are life to those who find them, and health to all their flesh.

23 Keep your heart with all diligence, for out of it spring the issues of life.

24 Put away from you a deceitful mouth, and put perverse lips far from you.

25 Let your eyes look straight ahead, and your eyelids look right before you.

26 Ponder the path of your feet, and let all your ways be established.

27 Do not turn to the right or the left; remove your foot from evil.

ord, I decide to pursue Your wisdom and understanding today. It is valuable to me. Help me to never abandon wisdom because it will protect and promote me. I want my love for wisdom to grow, so I decide to make wisdom a priority in my life. And along with wisdom, Lord, help me to gain understanding of Your Word and obey it.

It's wonderful to know that when You are directing my steps on the right path, my steps are not hindered. I can run and not stumble.

Without hesitation, I choose to receive Your instructions and not let go for any reason. As I receive and hear Your sayings, I will live longer. They bring life to me!

Steer me away from the path of the wicked. I choose to avoid it completely. Instead, I will turn from it and go in the opposite direction. Lord, help me to see today that the path of the just is like a shining light. The longer I stay on it the brighter it gets, but the path of the wicked is dark. So help me, Lord, to follow Your Word. Fine-tune my ears to hear what You have to say.

Because I love Your Word so much, I commit to read and receive it deep within my heart today. This brings life and health to my whole being.

Help me to guard my heart at all times because it affects every area of my life. Lord, keep me from saying deceptive and vulgar words.

Are there words that I say that are profane or deceitful? Lord, if there are, please deliver me from them. Keep me focused on what is right. Remove every distraction from my life. Help me to think seriously about the path I have chosen. Direct me so I can place all of my steps in the right direction. Today, I determine to stick to Your path and stay away from evil.

# CHAPTER 5

1 My son, pay attention to my wisdom; lend your ear to my understanding,

2 That you may preserve discretion, and your lips may keep knowledge.

3 For the lips of an immoral woman drip honey, and her mouth is smoother than oil;

4 But in the end she is bitter as wormwood, sharp as a two-edged sword.

5 Her feet go down to death, her steps lay hold of hell.

6 Lest you ponder her path of life—her ways are unstable; you do not know them.

7 Therefore hear me now, my children, and do not depart from the words of my mouth.

8 Remove your way far from her, and do not go near the door of her house,

9 Lest you give your honor to others, and your years to the cruel one;

10 Lest aliens be filled with your wealth, and your labors go to the house of a foreigner;

11 And you mourn at last, when your flesh and your body are consumed,

12 And say: "How I have hated instruction, and my heart despised correction!

13 I have not obeyed the voice of my teachers, nor inclined my ear to those who instructed me!

14 I was on the verge of total ruin, in the midst of the assembly and congregation."

15 Drink water from your own cistern, and running water from your own well.

16 Should your fountains be dispersed abroad, streams of water in the streets?

17 Let them be only your own, and not for strangers with you.

18 Let your fountain be blessed, and rejoice with the wife of your youth.

19 As a loving deer and a graceful doe, let her breasts satisfy you at all times; and always be enraptured with her love.

20 For why should you, my son, be enraptured by an immoral woman, and be embraced in the arms of a seductress?

21 For the ways of man are before the eyes of the LORD, and He ponders all his paths.

22 His own iniquities entrap the wicked man, and he is caught in the cords of his sin.

23 He shall die for lack of instruction, and in the greatness of his folly he shall go astray.

# C H A P T E R 5
## P R A Y E R

ord, I choose today to pay close attention to wisdom and listen intently to understanding. By doing so, I will exercise discretion, and what I say will be wise and full of knowledge.

Keep me from sexually immoral people today. Their words may be smooth, but their ways are more destructive than a two-edged sword. The path they want to take me down only leads to death and hell. I decide today not to follow that path. I won't even consider choosing their ways. Instead, I will run from them and stay away from where they are. For I know, Lord, that if I ever go that way, I can lose my wealth and bring shame into my life. My honor will go to others and years of productivity will be lost. Therefore, I choose to rejoice with the wife (husband) of my youth. Thank You for her (his) love. I celebrate her (him), and choose to be sexually faithful to only her (him).

Lord, what immoral people are trying to influence my life today? I pray that You would show me who they are and deliver me from them.

I know that everywhere I go and in everything I do, You see what is going on. You are watching me closely. You are weighing and considering my daily choices.

Lord, I don't want to be like the wicked man who ends up doomed by his own sins, trapped in what he has done. I want to live a life free, in You. Thank You for Your instruction and truth today.

Prov. 3:5-6

Trust in the Lord with all your heart,

and lean not on your own understanding;

In all your ways acknowledge Him,

and He shall direct

your paths.

1   My son, if you become surety for your friend, if you have shaken hands in pledge for a stranger,

2   You are snared by the words of your mouth; you are taken by the words of your mouth.

3   So do this, my son, and deliver yourself; for you have come into the hand of your friend: go and humble yourself; plead with your friend.

4   Give no sleep to your eyes, nor slumber to your eyelids.

5   Deliver yourself like a gazelle from the hand of the hunter, and like a bird from the hand of the fowler.

6   Go to the ant, you sluggard! Consider her ways and be wise,

7   Which, having no captain, overseer or ruler,

8   Provides her supplies in the summer, and gathers her food in the harvest.

9   How long will you slumber, O sluggard? When will you rise from your sleep?

10  A little sleep, a little slumber, a little folding of the hands to sleep—

11  So shall your poverty come on you like a prowler, and your need like an armed man.

12  A worthless person, a wicked man, walks with a perverse mouth;

13  He winks with his eyes, he shuffles his feet, he points with his fingers;

14  Perversity is in his heart, he devises evil continually, he sows discord.

15  Therefore his calamity shall come suddenly; suddenly he shall be broken without remedy.

16  These six things the LORD hates, yes, seven are an abomination to Him:

17  A proud look, a lying tongue, hands that shed innocent blood,

18 A heart that devises wicked plans, feet that are swift in running to evil,

19 A false witness who speaks lies, and one who sows discord among brethren.

20 My son, keep your father's command, and do not forsake the law of your mother.

21 Bind them continually upon your heart; Tie them around your neck.

22 When you roam, they will lead you; when you sleep, they will keep you; and when you awake, they will speak with you.

23 For the commandment is a lamp, and the law a light; reproofs of instruction are the way of life,

24 To keep you from the evil woman, from the flattering tongue of a seductress.

25 Do not lust after her beauty in your heart, nor let her allure you with her eyelids.

26 For by means of a harlot a man is reduced to a crust of bread; and an adulteress will prey upon his precious life.

27 Can a man take fire to his bosom, and his clothes not be burned?

28 Can one walk on hot coals, and his feet not be seared?

29 So is he who goes in to his neighbor's wife; whoever touches her shall not be innocent.

30 People do not despise a thief if he steals to satisfy himself when he is starving.

31 Yet when he is found, he must restore sevenfold; he may have to give up all the substance of his house.

32 Whoever commits adultery with a woman lacks understanding; he who does so destroys his own soul.

33 Wounds and dishonor he will get, and his reproach will not be wiped away.

34 For jealousy is a husband's fury; therefore he will not spare in the day of vengeance.

35 He will accept no recompense, nor will he be appeased though you give many gifts.

# CHAPTER 6
## PRAYER

ord, lead me so I can be wise in my financial matters today. Keep me from being a guarantor on a loan for another person. Keep me away from this kind of trouble. I don't want to be trapped by making a foolish agreement. Help me today to consider what I say because I know that I can become literally snared by what I say.

Thank You for creating the ant, Lord. Because You have presented them as an example, I want to learn from their ways and become wise. They work hard and do things in the right season. When they need something, their resources are always there because they are diligent in their work. Deliver me from being a lazy person. Help me to see how the productive ways of the ant can teach me to be wise.

Are there any areas I am lazy in, Lord? Please reveal them to me. I don't want to be lazy because poverty can creep up on me like a robber and steal from me. Help me to be diligent today.

Open my eyes to see wrong associations in my life. Remove and keep them away from me. I don't want naughty, wicked, and ungodly people hanging around my life. Deliver me from liars and those who are deceptive in everything they do. Keep me from people who are thinking up new ways to take advantage of others and from those who stir up trouble everywhere they go. Show me who these people are so I can avoid them. Thank You that I will not find myself in a hopeless situation, full of trouble, because of wrong associations in my life.

Free me from these things that are an abomination to You: a proud look, a lying tongue, hands that take advantage of the innocent, a heart that invents wicked ideas, feet that hurry to sin, a lying witness and a person who causes strife among people who were close to each other.

Lord, I honor my parents' instruction today because they can help and guide me. I thank You for Your Holy Spirit who helps me to be an honest person and gives me discernment when others are telling lies.

Deliver me today, Lord, from any lust I have towards others. Help me turn my eyes away from any destructive temptation. I won't take lustful fire into my heart. I know that this kind of behavior is simply dumb because it destroys my soul.

Lord, Your commandment is a lamp, and Your law is light in my life. Thank You for keeping me from evil people and safe from their crafty words.

# CHAPTER 7

1   My son, keep my words, and treasure my commands within you.

2   Keep my commands and live, and my law as the apple of your eye.

3   Bind them on your fingers; write them on the tablet of your heart.

4   Say to wisdom, "You are my sister," and call understanding your nearest kin,

5   That they may keep you from the immoral woman, from the seductress who flatters with her words.

6   For at the window of my house I looked through my lattice,

7   And saw among the simple, I perceived among the youths, a young man devoid of understanding,

8   Passing along the street near her corner; and he took the path to her house

9   In the twilight, in the evening, in the black and dark night.

10  And there a woman met him, with the attire of a harlot, and a crafty heart.

11  She was loud and rebellious, her feet would not stay at home.

12  At times she was outside, at times in the open square, Lurking at every corner.

13  So she caught him and kissed him; with an impudent face she said to him:

14  "I have peace offerings with me; today I have paid my vows.

15  So I came out to meet you, diligently to seek your face, and I have found you.

16  I have spread my bed with tapestry, Colored coverings of Egyptian linen.

17  I have perfumed my bed with myrrh, aloes, and cinnamon.

18  Come, let us take our fill of love until morning; let us delight ourselves with love.

19  For my husband is not at home; he has gone on a long journey;

20  He has taken a bag of money with him, and will come home on the appointed day."

21  With her enticing speech she caused him to yield, with her flattering lips she seduced him.

22  Immediately he went after her, as an ox goes to the slaughter, or as a fool to the correction of the stocks,

23  Till an arrow struck his liver. As a bird hastens to the snare, he did not know it would cost his life.

24  Now therefore, listen to me, my children; pay attention to the words of my mouth:

25  Do not let your heart turn aside to her ways, do not stray into her paths;

26  For she has cast down many wounded, and all who were slain by her were strong men.

27  Her house is the way to hell, descending to the chambers of death.

# CHAPTER 7
## PRAYER

ord, I want to keep Your Words and capture Your commandments deep within me today. Doing this frees me to live a wonderful life. Your Word is the greatest thing in my life. It is the apple of my eye. It's so incredibly precious that I eagerly receive it deep within my heart. I choose to see, know and understand everything from Your perspective.

Are there any areas of my life that I am viewing from a human perspective and not Yours, Lord? Teach me what Your Word says about those areas so I can acquire Your perspective today.

I love wisdom, so today I say to wisdom, "You are my sister." I'm going to thankfully declare that understanding is my close friend. I know that as I do this, it will keep me away from wrong men and women. In fact, I'm going to let Your wisdom help keep me from wrong people and their flattery every day.

I know that no person is immune to temptation. So, I will learn from the story of the evil woman these important truths: I will resist the lure of association with sexually immoral people, especially when they speak enticing words. Instead, I will turn from them and listen to Your Words. I won't let my heart be pulled towards them. Like an oxen going to slaughter, many strong people have been taken down and ruined by yielding to them. The road they want me to travel along only leads to hell and death. I choose holiness today. I say no to lust.

Thank You, Lord, for caring so much for me.

Prov. 13:20

He who walks with wise men will be wise,

but the companion of fools

will be destroyed.

# CHAPTER 8

1  Does not wisdom cry out, and understanding lift up her voice?
2  She takes her stand on the top of the high hill, beside the way, where the paths meet.
3  She cries out by the gates, at the entry of the city, at the entrance of the doors:
4  "To you, O men, I call, and my voice is to the sons of men.
5  O you simple ones, understand prudence, and you fools, be of an understanding heart.
6  Listen, for I will speak of excellent things, and from the opening of my lips will come right things;
7  For my mouth will speak truth; wickedness is an abomination to my lips.
8  All the words of my mouth are with righteousness; nothing crooked or perverse is in them.
9  They are all plain to him who understands, and right to those who find knowledge.
10  Receive my instruction, and not silver, and knowledge rather than choice gold;
11  For wisdom is better than rubies, and all the things one may desire cannot be compared with her.
12  "I, wisdom, dwell with prudence, and find out knowledge and discretion.
13  The fear of the LORD is to hate evil; pride and arrogance and the evil way and the perverse mouth I hate.
14  Counsel is mine, and sound wisdom; I am understanding, I have strength.
15  By me kings reign, and rulers decree justice.
16  By me princes rule, and nobles, all the judges of the earth.
17  I love those who love me, and those who seek me diligently will find me.
18  Riches and honor are with me, enduring riches and righteousness.

19 My fruit is better than gold, yes, than fine gold, and my revenue than choice silver.
20 I traverse the way of righteousness, in the midst of the paths of justice,
21 That I may cause those who love me to inherit wealth, that I may fill their treasuries.
22 "The LORD possessed me at the beginning of His way, before His works of old.
23 I have been established from everlasting, from the beginning, before there was ever an earth.
24 When there were no depths I was brought forth, when there were no fountains abounding with water.
25 Before the mountains were settled, before the hills, I was brought forth;
26 While as yet He had not made the earth or the fields, or the primeval dust of the world.
27 When He prepared the heavens, I was there, when He drew a circle on the face of the deep,
28 When He established the clouds above, when He strengthened the fountains of the deep,
29 When He assigned to the sea its limit, so that the waters would not transgress His command, when He marked out the foundations of the earth,
30 Then I was beside Him as a master craftsman; and I was daily His delight, rejoicing always before Him,
31 Rejoicing in His inhabited world, and my delight was with the sons of men.
32 "Now therefore, listen to me, my children, for blessed are those who keep my ways.
33 Hear instruction and be wise, and do not disdain it.
34 Blessed is the man who listens to me, watching daily at my gates, waiting at the posts of my doors.
35 For whoever finds me finds life, and obtains favor from the LORD;
36 But he who sins against me wrongs his own soul; all those who hate me love death."

ord, fine-tune my ears to hear what wisdom and understanding have to say. Help me understand today that wisdom has important information for me and gives me common sense. When I look for wisdom, I can find it. It helps me to be a better leader and it is infinitely more valuable than the best silver or gold. So, God, I ask for Your wisdom in every area of my life.

Today, I receive Your instruction and knowledge because it is valuable. Thank You that as I apply Your sound wisdom, it will help me make the right decisions.

I choose to respect and fear You today. I choose to hate evil.

Create in me a distaste for pride, arrogance, corruption, deceit, evil ideas, and wrong words. Instead, help me receive the good advice and the common sense of Your wisdom. It is because of wisdom's help that leaders are effective.

Wisdom says, "I love those who love me, and those that seek me early find me." Please, lead me today to seek Your wisdom with all my heart.

Thank You that prosperity naturally follows Your wisdom and that finances and honor can come into my life. Abundance that lasts a long time comes as a result of Your wisdom. So, Lord, I want to receive all that You have for me. I trust in You.

The result of following Your way and judgment is better than having fine gold. Those who love and follow You are the wealthiest of all. When I hear Your instructions, I know I'll be wise.

Thank You, Lord, that Your wisdom has been here from the very beginning. It existed before the earth began. Yes, even when You established the heavens, wisdom was there. Wisdom was here when You marked out the foundations of the earth and was Your constant delight.

Is there any area of my life where I am refusing Your instruction today, Lord? I know that I'm blessed when I keep Your ways, so I decide to keep Your ways today and receive Your blessings in my life.

# CHAPTER 9

1  Wisdom has built her house, she has hewn out her seven pillars;

2  She has slaughtered her meat, she has mixed her wine, she has also furnished her table.

3  She has sent out her maidens, she cries out from the highest places of the city,

4  "Whoever is simple, let him turn in here!" As for him who lacks understanding, she says to him,

5  "Come, eat of my bread and drink of the wine I have mixed.

6  Forsake foolishness and live, and go in the way of understanding.

7  "He who corrects a scoffer gets shame for himself, and he who rebukes a wicked man only harms himself.

8  Do not correct a scoffer, lest he hate you; rebuke a wise man, and he will love you.

9  Give instruction to a wise man, and he will be still wiser; teach a just man, and he will increase in learning.

10  "The fear of the LORD is the beginning of wisdom, and the knowledge of the Holy One is understanding.

11  For by me your days will be multiplied, and years of life will be added to you.

12  If you are wise, you are wise for yourself, and if you scoff, you will bear it alone."

13  A foolish woman is clamorous; she is simple, and knows nothing.

14 For she sits at the door of her house, on a seat by the highest places of the city,

15 To call to those who pass by, who go straight on their way:

16 "Whoever is simple, let him turn in here"; and as for him who lacks understanding, she says to him,

17 "Stolen water is sweet, and bread eaten in secret is pleasant."

18 But he does not know that the dead are there, that her guests are in the depths of hell.

ord, today I understand that wisdom is strong, calling me to come and receive. Your wisdom invites me to understand Your truth and ways. I decide to pursue Your wisdom and truth.

I choose to turn my back on foolish things and live Your way. Is there any foolish thing I have allowed to come into my life? I ask You to remove it from me today and help me grow in spiritual things.

Today, I will not waste my time trying to correct someone who mocks others. Instead, let me become wise by receiving correction from a wise person. Thank You for opportunities to work with wise people today and for the privilege of assisting them in becoming even wiser. It's wonderful knowing that You bring every kind of understanding into my life as my knowledge of You grows. I want to know You more today, Lord.

Lord, I recognize that the fear of You is the beginning of wisdom, so I pray that my fear of You will grow. I want to receive all of Your wisdom today. I know it makes every hour of my day more profitable and makes the years of my life abundant and fruitful. Wisdom is its own reward, and brings long life to me. Help me to receive Your direction today.

Help me steer clear of immoral people today. I will be alert to their sweet words, knowing that those who have been with them before are now citizens in hell. These type of people don't bring life; they destroy the ignorant who blindly walk into their traps.

Prov. 26:12

Do you see a man wise

in his own eyes?

There is more hope

for a fool than for him.

# CHAPTER 10

1 The proverbs of Solomon: a wise son makes a glad father, but a foolish son is the grief of his mother.

2 Treasures of wickedness profit nothing, but righteousness delivers from death.

3 The LORD will not allow the righteous soul to famish, but He casts away the desire of the wicked.

4 He who has a slack hand becomes poor, but the hand of the diligent makes rich.

5 He who gathers in summer is a wise son, but he who sleeps in harvest is a son who causes shame.

6 Blessings are on the head of the righteous, but violence covers the mouth of the wicked.

7 The memory of the righteous is blessed, but the name of the wicked will rot.

8 The wise in heart will receive commands, but a prating fool will fall.

9 He who walks with integrity walks securely, but he who perverts his ways will become known.

10 He who winks with the eye causes trouble, but a prating fool will fall.

11 The mouth of the righteous is a well of life, but violence covers the mouth of the wicked.

12 Hatred stirs up strife, but love covers all sins.

13 Wisdom is found on the lips of him who has understanding, but a rod is for the back of him who is devoid of understanding.

14 Wise people store up knowledge, but the mouth of the foolish is near destruction.

15 The rich man's wealth is his strong city; the destruction of the poor is their poverty.

16 The labor of the righteous leads to life, the wages of the wicked to sin.

17 He who keeps instruction is in the way of life, but he who refuses correction goes astray.

18 Whoever hides hatred has lying lips, and whoever spreads slander is a fool.

19 In the multitude of words sin is not lacking, but he who restrains his lips is wise.

20 The tongue of the righteous is choice silver; the heart of the wicked is worth little.

21 The lips of the righteous feed many, but fools die for lack of wisdom.

22 The blessing of the LORD makes one rich, and He adds no sorrow with it.

23 To do evil is like sport to a fool, but a man of understanding has wisdom.

24 The fear of the wicked will come upon him, and the desire of the righteous will be granted.

25 When the whirlwind passes by, the wicked is no more, but the righteous has an everlasting foundation.

26 As vinegar to the teeth and smoke to the eyes, so is the lazy man to those who send him.

27 The fear of the LORD prolongs days, but the years of the wicked will be shortened.

28 The hope of the righteous will be gladness, but the expectation of the wicked will perish.

29 The way of the LORD is strength for the upright, but destruction will come to the workers of iniquity.

30 The righteous will never be removed, but the wicked will not inhabit the earth.

31 The mouth of the righteous brings forth wisdom, but the perverse tongue will be cut out.

32 The lips of the righteous know what is acceptable, but the mouth of the wicked what is perverse.

# CHAPTER 10
## PRAYER

ord, thank You for showing me today that ill-gotten gain brings no lasting happiness. You always take care of those who do what is right. Help me today to live in faithful obedience. Thank You for giving me the resolve to live steadfastly as a person who doesn't give up easily. Today I choose to be diligent. As I do, You prosper me.

Help me find Your divine timing today so I can produce the greatest results at the most opportune time. I don't want to miss my hour of opportunity. I want to be in the middle of Your will.

I decide to be wise by receiving Your commandments and instructions. Help me understand that when I feel self-sufficient, I'm ripe for mistakes. Today I choose to walk in integrity and be confident as a result.

I'll not take sin lightly, because it brings sorrow to my life. Remove any hatred I have towards others because this kind of attitude brings strife. And thank You, Lord, that love covers all sins.

Lord, help me to hold my tongue today. Help me to sincerely consider everything I say. Convict me if I'm inclined to pour out everything I know, because continuous talking can lead to all kinds of problems.

Help me to be teachable in everything I do today. I know that as I am, I'll be on the pathway to a productive and accurate life.

Lord, I know that only fools slander, so help me refrain from doing that today. If someone invites me to speak against another, help me keep from talking so much and putting my foot in my mouth. Instead, let me be sensible, and stop. Please remind me to say right, life-giving words. When I do, they will be more valuable than silver to those who hear. Send opportunities to me so I can give good advice to help others today.

Help me lead others to Your wisdom today. I want to be an example of that truth today with those who don't know You. Only Your blessings can bring prosperity without any negative results.

A fool's fun is doing mischief, but a wise person's fun is being wise. So help me today, Lord, to be wise. Teach me to be an excellent employee, never lazy, and a joy to those who work with me. Is there any way I can do a better job at work today, Lord? How can I treat those who work with me better?

Lord, I see that the desires of good people will be met, but the wicked will lose everything. Your way brings strength to me, and by fearing You I'll live longer.

# CHAPTER 11

1   Dishonest scales are an abomination to the LORD, but a just weight is His delight.

2   When pride comes, then comes shame; but with the humble is wisdom.

3   The integrity of the upright will guide them, but the perversity of the unfaithful will destroy them.

4   Riches do not profit in the day of wrath, but righteousness delivers from death.

5   The righteousness of the blameless will direct his way aright, but the wicked will fall by his own wickedness.

6   The righteousness of the upright will deliver them, but the unfaithful will be caught by their lust.

7   When a wicked man dies, his expectation will perish, and the hope of the unjust perishes.

8   The righteous is delivered from trouble, and it comes to the wicked instead.

9   The hypocrite with his mouth destroys his neighbor, but through knowledge the righteous will be delivered.

10  When it goes well with the righteous, the city rejoices; and when the wicked perish, there is jubilation.

11  By the blessing of the upright the city is exalted, but it is over-thrown by the mouth of the wicked.

12  He who is devoid of wisdom despises his neighbor, but a man of understanding holds his peace.

13  A talebearer reveals secrets, but he who is of a faithful spirit conceals a matter.

14  Where there is no counsel, the people fall; but in the multitude of counselors there is safety.

15  He who is surety for a stranger will suffer, but one who hates being surety is secure.

16 A gracious woman retains honor, but ruthless men retain riches.

17 The merciful man does good for his own soul, but he who is cruel troubles his own flesh.

18 The wicked man does deceptive work, but he who sows righteousness will have a sure reward.

19 As righteousness leads to life, so he who pursues evil pursues it to his own death.

20 Those who are of a perverse heart are an abomination to the LORD, but the blameless in their ways are His delight.

21 Though they join forces, the wicked will not go unpunished; but the posterity of the righteous will be delivered.

22 As a ring of gold in a swine's snout, so is a lovely woman who lacks discretion.

23 The desire of the righteous is only good, but the expectation of the wicked is wrath.

24 There is one who scatters, yet increases more; and there is one who withholds more than is right, but it leads to poverty.

25 The generous soul will be made rich, and he who waters will also be watered himself.

26 The people will curse him who withholds grain, but blessing will be on the head of him who sells it.

27 He who earnestly seeks good finds favor, but trouble will come to him who seeks evil.

28 He who trusts in his riches will fall, but the righteous will flourish like foliage.

29 He who troubles his own house will inherit the wind, and the fool will be servant to the wise of heart.

30 The fruit of the righteous is a tree of life, and he who wins souls is wise.

31 If the righteous will be recompensed on the earth, how much more the ungodly and the sinner.

# CHAPTER 11
## PRAYER

 choose to be accurate in everything I do today. I will not cheat. I want to be completely honest, because I know that You delight in honesty. Remove pride from me today because a proud person finishes in shame. I choose to be humble. The humble receive Your wisdom.

Lord, help me to be a person of integrity because it guides me in the right way to go. Let me see that evil people are destroyed by their dishonesty. Help me gain the right perspective through knowing that only righteousness will count on Judgment Day and that riches will be of no help.

Help me to do what is right because righteousness will deliver me. I want to say only right words today because evil words destroy. So, Lord, help me watch my mouth. Keep me from quarreling with my neighbors. Help me to hold my tongue. Remove from me any gossiping or spreading of rumors.

I know I receive Your safety by surrounding myself with many counselors. I ask You to bring people into my life who are full of good counsel so I will not fall.

Open my eyes to see that I should not offer to guarantee a debt for another person. Help me understand that it's better to say "no" than to reap the consequences later.

When I'm merciful to others it nourishes my own soul. Help me to be merciful and not cruel because those who are cruel to others destroy their own soul. Today, I want to sow righteousness because it rewards my life forever.

Help me stay clear from the paths of evil today. Instead, I want to do the right thing and bring increase to my life. I want to find life, not death.

Show me how to be a person of discretion and modesty in everything I say and do. Keep me from being stubborn in my heart towards You. I want to be a delight to You as an upright and good person.

Help me always to be a person who gives away instead of one who holds on too tightly. I thank You that when I give, I become richer. If I hold on too tightly, I can lose everything. By helping others, I help myself. So Lord, help me to become a liberal giver. Remove from me any faith I have in my own riches because it will only bring failure.

As I trust in You today, I will grow and flourish. I will diligently seek good. When I do, I'll receive Your favor. I refuse to seek and follow after mischief because I don't want it coming back after me.

Help me to be a godly person today, Lord, growing like a tree that gives out life-giving fruit. Help me win souls for You.

# CHAPTER 12

1 Whoever loves instruction loves knowledge, but he who hates correction is stupid.

2 A good man obtains favor from the LORD, but a man of wicked intentions He will condemn.

3 A man is not established by wickedness, but the root of the righteous cannot be moved.

4 An excellent wife is the crown of her husband, but she who causes shame is like rottenness in his bones.

5 The thoughts of the righteous are right, but the counsels of the wicked are deceitful.

6 The words of the wicked are, "Lie in wait for blood," but the mouth of the upright will deliver them.

7 The wicked are overthrown and are no more, but the house of the righteous will stand.

8 A man will be commended according to his wisdom, but he who is of a perverse heart will be despised.

9 Better is the one who is slighted but has a servant, than he who honors himself but lacks bread.

10 A righteous man regards the life of his animal, but the tender mercies of the wicked are cruel.

11 He who tills his land will be satisfied with bread, but he who follows frivolity is devoid of understanding.

12 The wicked covet the catch of evil men, but the root of the righteous yields fruit.

13 The wicked is ensnared by the transgression of his lips, but the righteous will come through trouble.

14 A man will be satisfied with good by the fruit of his mouth, and the recompense of a man's hands will be rendered to him.

15 The way of a fool is right in his own eyes, but he who heeds counsel is wise.

16 A fool's wrath is known at once, but a prudent man covers shame.

17 He who speaks truth declares righteousness, but a false witness, deceit.

18 There is one who speaks like the piercings of a sword, but the tongue of the wise promotes health.

19 The truthful lip shall be established forever, but a lying tongue is but for a moment.

20 Deceit is in the heart of those who devise evil, but counselors of peace have joy.

21 No grave trouble will overtake the righteous, but the wicked shall be filled with evil.

22 Lying lips are an abomination to the LORD, but those who deal truthfully are His delight.

23 A prudent man conceals knowledge, but the heart of fools proclaims foolishness.

24 The hand of the diligent will rule, but the lazy man will be put to forced labor.

25 Anxiety in the heart of man causes depression, but a good word makes it glad.

26 The righteous should choose his friends carefully, for the way of the wicked leads them astray.

27 The lazy man does not roast what he took in hunting, but diligence is man's precious possession.

28 In the way of righteousness is life, and in its pathway there is no death.

# CHAPTER 12
## PRAYER

each me to love instruction and knowledge today, Lord. Don't let me turn my back on correction because when I do, I'm simply stupid.

Thank You for Your favor that blesses my life when I seek to be a good person. Thank You for showing me that a life lived only in righteousness has a solid foundation. Help me understand today that wickedness and evil will never bring real success.

Fill my mind with right and honest thoughts today. Remove from me the counsel of wicked people that is full of lies and deceit. Deliver me from a perverse heart. Fill my life with Your wisdom.

I choose to work hard and be able to provide. I know that hard work brings blessing and only a fool wastes time. Lord, are there any areas I can work on more diligently today?

Help me to say the right thing. Keep me from lies that get me into trouble. Instead, let my honesty speak for itself and deliver me.

Lord, please don't let me foolishly think that I'll never need any good advice. Help me see the error when I try to be right in my own eyes. Rather, let me receive good counsel and become wise. Help me listen to others and gain wisdom.

Help me today, Lord, not to be quick-tempered. I don't want anger to dominate my life. Instead, I choose to be thoughtful, always keeping my cool when trouble is all around. Today, I decide to speak the truth and do the right thing.

Help me to avoid saying things today that might hurt other people. I decide now to say good words that bring others blessing, healing and peace.

Thank You, Father, that Your truth always outlives a lie. A lie may win in the short-run but it never lasts long because the truth endures forever. So remove from me any area of deceit and thoughts of evil so I will not be an abomination to You. Instead, let me be a person of peace and joy who is full of plans for good. Help me to deal truly and accurately in everything I do today. No matter what the circumstances, help me keep my promises and my word so I will be Your delight.

Help me to live a godly life so I will have no fear of death. I will work hard and smart today. I want to be the most diligent person I know. So Father, please remove any area of laziness, heaviness, or anxiousness in my heart.

# CHAPTER 13

1  A wise son heeds his father's instruction, but a scoffer does not listen to rebuke.

2  A man shall eat well by the fruit of his mouth, but the soul of the unfaithful feeds on violence.

3  He who guards his mouth preserves his life, but he who opens wide his lips shall have destruction.

4  The soul of a lazy man desires, and has nothing; but the soul of the diligent shall be made rich.

5  A righteous man hates lying, but a wicked man is loathsome and comes to shame.

6  Righteousness keeps him whose way is blameless, but wickedness overthrows the sinner.

7  There is one who makes himself rich, yet has nothing; and one who makes himself poor, yet has great riches.

8  The ransom of a man's life is his riches, but the poor does not hear rebuke.

9  The light of the righteous rejoices, but the lamp of the wicked will be put out.

10  By pride comes nothing but strife, but with the well-advised is wisdom.

11  Wealth gained by dishonesty will be diminished, but he who gathers by labor will increase.

12  Hope deferred makes the heart sick, but when the desire comes, it is a tree of life.

13 He who despises the word will be destroyed, but he who fears the commandment will be rewarded.

14 The law of the wise is a fountain of life, to turn one away from the snares of death.

15 Good understanding gains favor, but the way of the unfaithful is hard.

16 Every prudent man acts with knowledge, but a fool lays open his folly.

17 A wicked messenger falls into trouble, but a faithful ambassador brings health.

18 Poverty and shame will come to him who disdains correction, but he who regards a rebuke will be honored.

19 A desire accomplished is sweet to the soul, but it is an abomination to fools to depart from evil.

20 He who walks with wise men will be wise, but the companion of fools will be destroyed.

21 Evil pursues sinners, but to the righteous, good shall be repaid.

22 A good man leaves an inheritance to his children's children, but the wealth of the sinner is stored up for the righteous.

23 Much food is in the fallow ground of the poor, and for lack of justice there is waste.

24 He who spares his rod hates his son, but he who loves him disciplines him promptly.

25 The righteous eats to the satisfying of his soul, but the stomach of the wicked shall be in want.

# CHAPTER 13
## PRAYER

hank You, Lord, for helping me say the right words. When they come out of my mouth, they produce good fruit in my life. Remove from me an argumentative or evil vocabulary. Show me today when to keep my mouth shut and how to control my tongue. Keep me from verbally reacting to others. Thank You that when I do this, You will keep my life and remove destruction from me.

Remove slothfulness and laziness from my life today, Lord. Don't let mediocrity rule my life. Today, I choose to be a diligent person, working hard and showing increase in my life. Thank You for promising to prosper me when I live my life this way.

I want to be a righteous person the rest of my life. I decide today to hate lies and inaccuracies. Keep me from being evil and harming myself by my own wickedness. Remove pride from my life today because it only leads to arguments, strife and contention.

Lord, in what areas of my life does pride have a grip on me? Please show me. Help me to be humble and receive good counsel this week so I will become wiser and gain wisdom.

Keep me from situations that indefinitely postpone what I'm hoping for because it makes my heart sick. Let me understand today that there is no greater reward than to hold fast and true to Your will and Your Word. I choose to never disregard or reject Your Word and become destroyed. Instead, I will fear Your commandments, obey them and succeed.

Today, I will actively pursue and receive the advice of wise people. As I do, it will refresh me and become a fountain of life to me, keeping me aware and away from pitfalls and problems that lie ahead.

Lord, teach me to be thoughtful in everything that I do. Direct me in how to think and plan ahead. Help me to receive good instruction in every area of my life. I decide to listen and receive the right kinds of correction today, because as I do, You will bring honor into my life and remove poverty and shame.

Lord, I thank You for right associations in my life. I only want to walk with wise people, because as I do, I'll become wiser and wiser. Help me recognize and disconnect from any foolish companions in my life.

Help me to improve my parenting skills today, Lord. Never let me be afraid of disciplining my children. Thank You for the love I show them when I am faithful to correct.

1    The wise woman builds her house, but the foolish pulls it down with her hands.

2    He who walks in his uprightness fears the LORD, but he who is perverse in his ways despises Him.

3    In the mouth of a fool is a rod of pride, but the lips of the wise will preserve them.

4    Where no oxen are, the trough is clean; but much increase comes by the strength of an ox.

5    A faithful witness does not lie, but a false witness will utter lies.

6    A scoffer seeks wisdom and does not find it, but knowledge is easy to him who understands.

7    Go from the presence of a foolish man, when you do not perceive in him the lips of knowledge.

8    The wisdom of the prudent is to understand his way, but the folly of fools is deceit.

9    Fools mock at sin, but among the upright there is favor.

10   The heart knows its own bitterness, and a stranger does not share its joy.

11   The house of the wicked will be overthrown, but the tent of the upright will flourish.

12   There is a way that seems right to a man, but its end is the way of death.

13   Even in laughter the heart may sorrow, and the end of mirth may be grief.

14   The backslider in heart will be filled with his own ways, but a good man will be satisfied from above.

15   The simple believes every word, but the prudent considers well his steps.

16   A wise man fears and departs from evil, but a fool rages and is self-confident.

17   A quick-tempered man acts foolishly, and a man of wicked intentions is hated.

18 The simple inherit folly, but the prudent are crowned with knowledge.
19 The evil will bow before the good, and the wicked at the gates of the righteous.
20 The poor man is hated even by his own neighbor, but the rich has many friends.
21 He who despises his neighbor sins; but he who has mercy on the poor, happy is he.
22 Do they not go astray who devise evil? But mercy and truth belong to those who devise good.
23 In all labor there is profit, but idle chatter leads only to poverty.
24 The crown of the wise is their riches, but the foolishness of fools is folly.
25 A true witness delivers souls, but a deceitful witness speaks lies.
26 In the fear of the LORD there is strong confidence, and His children will have a place of refuge.
27 The fear of the LORD is a fountain of life, to turn one away from the snares of death.
28 In a multitude of people is a king's honor, but in the lack of people is the downfall of a prince.
29 He who is slow to wrath has great understanding, but he who is impulsive exalts folly.
30 A sound heart is life to the body, but envy is rottenness to the bones.
31 He who oppresses the poor reproaches his Maker, but he who honors Him has mercy on the needy.
32 The wicked is banished in his wickedness, but the righteous has a refuge in his death.
33 Wisdom rests in the heart of him who has understanding, but what is in the heart of fools is made known.
34 Righteousness exalts a nation, but sin is a reproach to any people.
35 The king's favor is toward a wise servant, but his wrath is against him who causes shame.

# CHAPTER 14
## PRAYER

ord, I choose to walk right before You and honor You today. Deliver me from perversion, because that brings disgrace to You. Remove pride from me so my words won't become foolish. I want to say only wise things and receive Your protection.

Teach me today to be a truthful person. Remove any insults, criticism or skepticism I may harbor towards others. Instead, let me be a person of understanding. As I do, knowledge will easily come to me. Help me discern the truth when I am in the presence of foolish people. Let me be sensitive to what others say so that I'll know whether or not I should be around them.

Help me today to be prudent and consider every choice I make. Help me recognize any area of dishonesty in my life. I want to be honest and growing, instead of being wicked and defeated. Keep me from being wise in my own eyes and choosing my own ways. Direct me along Your path only.

Lord, is there something that I have been believing that I shouldn't believe today? Please reveal it to me so I can change. I want to be wise by being cautious and avoiding danger. I don't want to believe everything that I hear or see. Help me to consider every step I take.

Today, I choose to depart from every form of evil. Help me to avoid the foolishness of going full steam ahead trusting in the confidence of my own actions. Help me to stay free from anger, so I won't end up doing stupid things. Help me not to look down on others or ignore them. Instead, help me see with Your eyes and show mercy on the poor. Reveal new ways for me to help them. As I do, happiness will come into my life.

I refuse any temptation to plot evil against anyone today. Instead, I plan to do good. When I plan good things, mercy and truth will come into my life. Lord, help me to be a doer, not just a talker. If I only talk about situations, nothing happens. But if I work at it, there is a reward. So help me to say and do the right thing today, Lord. As I do, I will help other people.

Keep me from participating in foolishness. Remove from me the destructiveness of envy; I don't want to be jealous of others. Create in me a sound heart that gives me life.

Help me never to oppress the poor. Instead, I want to show them mercy.

Because I reverence You today, Lord, I have deep strength and strong confidence. Your confidence provides a place of refuge and a fountain of life to me. Thank You for this blessing.

# CHAPTER 15

1 A soft answer turns away wrath, but a harsh word stirs up anger.

2 The tongue of the wise uses knowledge rightly, but the mouth of fools pours forth foolishness.

3 The eyes of the LORD are in every place, keeping watch on the evil and the good.

4 A wholesome tongue is a tree of life, but perverseness in it breaks the spirit.

5 A fool despises his father's instruction, but he who receives correction is prudent.

6 In the house of the righteous there is much treasure, but in the revenue of the wicked is trouble.

7 The lips of the wise disperse knowledge, but the heart of the fool does not do so.

8 The sacrifice of the wicked is an abomination to the LORD, but the prayer of the upright is His delight.

9 The way of the wicked is an abomination to the LORD, but He loves him who follows righteousness.

10 Harsh discipline is for him who forsakes the way, and he who hates correction will die.

11 Hell and Destruction are before the LORD; so how much more the hearts of the sons of men.

12 A scoffer does not love one who corrects him, nor will he go to the wise.

13 A merry heart makes a cheerful countenance, but by sorrow of the heart the spirit is broken.

14 The heart of him who has understanding seeks knowledge, but the mouth of fools feeds on foolishness.

15 All the days of the afflicted are evil, but he who is of a merry heart has a continual feast.

16 Better is a little with the fear of the LORD, than great treasure with trouble.

17 Better is a dinner of herbs where love is, than a fatted calf with hatred.

18 A wrathful man stirs up strife, but he who is slow to anger allays contention.

19 The way of the lazy man is like a hedge of thorns, but the way of the upright is a highway.

20 A wise son makes a father glad, but a foolish man despises his mother.

21 Folly is joy to him who is destitute of discernment, but a man of understanding walks uprightly.

22 Without counsel, plans go awry, but in the multitude of counselors they are established.

23 A man has joy by the answer of his mouth, and a word spoken in due season, how good it is!

24 The way of life winds upward for the wise, that he may turn away from hell below.

25 The LORD will destroy the house of the proud, but He will establish the boundary of the widow.

26 The thoughts of the wicked are an abomination to the LORD, but the words of the pure are pleasant.

27 He who is greedy for gain troubles his own house, but he who hates bribes will live.

28 The heart of the righteous studies how to answer, but the mouth of the wicked pours forth evil.

29 The LORD is far from the wicked, but He hears the prayer of the righteous.

30 The light of the eyes rejoices the heart, and a good report makes the bones healthy.

31 The ear that hears the rebukes of life will abide among the wise.

32 He who disdains instruction despises his own soul, but he who heeds rebuke gets understanding.

33 The fear of the LORD is the instruction of wisdom, and before honor is humility.

ord, today, if I have an opportunity to be angry, help me to give a peaceful response instead. Keep me from saying hard or grievous words that stir up more anger.

I decide to have an attitude that makes learning a joy. Keep me from talking too much and saying every foolish thing I know. I know Your eyes are everywhere, seeing everything that I do and say.

Remove from me any ways of wickedness; I want to follow passionately after righteousness. Deliver me from being critical of others. Make me glad inside and let it show in my smile. Thank You, Lord, for giving me so much to be thankful for! Take away any sorrow in my heart that makes me want to give up.

Today, I will seek knowledge. I won't feed on foolishness. Help me to know, Lord, that a little is better with the fear of You than to have great wealth along with trouble. Help me to be righteous and not slothful, because the good way is like a highway and the lazy person's path is full of snares.

Today, I desire to be full of understanding and to live a holy life. I never want to lack Your wisdom. Please send people full of good advice into my life so my dreams and goals won't vanish. In fact, through many advisors they will be established.

Help me to be a person who says the right thing at the right time. Let me always choose Your way. Remove from my life any wicked thoughts or ideas so I will not be an abomination to You.

Lord, are there any thoughts I have had lately that aren't pleasing to You? If so, I ask You to deliver me from that kind of thinking. Instead, help me to be pure, speaking good and pleasant words.

Lord, help me stay free from greed to avoid troubling my own family. I will not receive any bribes today because they only lead to compromise. Help me to think before I respond to others. Remove from me any area of wickedness so You will stay close to me and hear my prayers.

Let my ears always be open to hear and receive the right kind of constructive criticism. Lord, keep me from refusing good and correct instruction. I know that if I accept wise criticism I will gain understanding, and then You will bring other wise people into my life.

# C H A P T E R 16

1 The preparations of the heart belong to man, but the answer of the tongue is from the LORD.
2 All the ways of a man are pure in his own eyes, but the LORD weighs the spirits.
3 Commit your works to the LORD, and your thoughts will be established.
4 The LORD has made all for Himself, yes, even the wicked for the day of doom.
5 Everyone proud in heart is an abomination to the LORD; though they join forces, none will go unpunished.
6 In mercy and truth atonement is provided for iniquity; and by the fear of the LORD one departs from evil.
7 When a man's ways please the LORD, he makes even his enemies to be at peace with him.
8 Better is a little with righteousness, than vast revenues without justice.
9 A man's heart plans his way, but the LORD directs his steps.
10 Divination is on the lips of the king; his mouth must not transgress in judgment.
11 Honest weights and scales are the LORD'S; all the weights in the bag are His work.
12 It is an abomination for kings to commit wickedness, for a throne is established by righteousness.
13 Righteous lips are the delight of kings, and they love him who speaks what is right.
14 As messengers of death is the king's wrath, but a wise man will appease it.
15 In the light of the king's face is life, and his favor is like a cloud of the latter rain.
16 How much better to get wisdom than gold! And to get

understanding is to be chosen rather than silver.

17 The highway of the upright is to depart from evil; he who keeps his way preserves his soul.

18 Pride goes before destruction, and a haughty spirit before a fall.

19 Better to be of a humble spirit with the lowly, than to divide the spoil with the proud.

20 He who heeds the word wisely will find good, and whoever trusts in the LORD, happy is he.

21 The wise in heart will be called prudent, and sweetness of the lips increases learning.

22 Understanding is a wellspring of life to him who has it. But the correction of fools is folly.

23 The heart of the wise teaches his mouth, and adds learning to his lips.

24 Pleasant words are like a honeycomb, sweetness to the soul and health to the bones.

25 There is a way that seems right to a man, but its end is the way of death.

26 The person who labors, labors for himself, for his hungry mouth drives him on.

27 An ungodly man digs up evil, and it is on his lips like a burning fire.

28 A perverse man sows strife, and a whisperer separates the best of friends.

29 A violent man entices his neighbor, and leads him in a way that is not good.

30 He winks his eye to devise perverse things; he purses his lips and brings about evil.

31 The silver-haired head is a crown of glory, if it is found in the way of righteousness.

32 He who is slow to anger is better than the mighty, and he who rules his spirit than he who takes a city.

33 The lot is cast into the lap, but its every decision is from the LORD.

# CHAPTER 16
## PRAYER

ord, thank You for showing me today that You've made everything for Your own purposes. I ask You today for what is good; not just what looks good. I choose to commit all my work to You. As I do, my thinking will become clear and accurate.

Remove any pride from my heart today so I won't be an abomination and disgust to You. Forgive me for any arrogance I have shown; I don't want to bring destruction to my life. Rather, help me to have a humble spirit because it is better to be humble with the poor than to be proud and with the rich.

I choose to reverence and fear You today. Doing this keeps me safe and causes evil to leave me. I choose to have all my ways please You. When I do, You cause my enemies to be at peace with me, and I thank You for that.

Lord, I have decided to gain Your wisdom and understanding because it is worth more than gold and fine silver. I will depend on You today to direct me when I make my plans. Help me to stay on the right path, far away from evil. Is there any path that I am presently taking that isn't right? Please show me the right way to go. I know that when I take the godly path I'll be safe and You will save my life.

I know, Lord, that anytime I trust in You, I will be happy and things will work out for the best. Therefore, I receive Your Word and choose to obey You today. Help me to have a wise heart and only use gracious, sweet words. When I do this, I increase my learning.

I want to let wisdom become a fountain of life to me. I want You to be a part of everything I do, so Lord, I invite You into every area of my life. Keep me from choosing the path that I, by myself, think is right. I want Your direction because I don't know everything. I need Your help in avoiding destruction that can come through a choice of my own.

Please keep me from digging up evil, sowing strife, and whispering gossip to my closest friends. I know this causes friendships to fall apart. I choose today never to gossip to my friends. Help me to rule my spirit today. Show me how to be slow-tempered and exhibit self-control.

# CHAPTER 17

1 Better is a dry morsel with quietness, than a house full of feasting with strife.

2 A wise servant will rule over a son who causes shame, and will share an inheritance among the brothers.

3 The refining pot is for silver and the furnace for gold, but the LORD tests the hearts.

4 An evildoer gives heed to false lips; a liar listens eagerly to a spiteful tongue.

5 He who mocks the poor reproaches his Maker; he who is glad at calamity will not go unpunished.

6 Children's children are the crown of old men, and the glory of children is their father.

7 Excellent speech is not becoming to a fool, much less lying lips to a prince.

8 A present is a precious stone in the eyes of its possessor; wherever he turns, he prospers.

9 He who covers a transgression seeks love, but he who repeats a matter separates friends.

10 Rebuke is more effective for a wise man than a hundred blows on a fool.

11 An evil man seeks only rebellion; therefore a cruel messenger will be sent against him.

12 Let a man meet a bear robbed of her cubs, rather than a fool in his folly.

13 Whoever rewards evil for good, evil will not depart from his house.

14 The beginning of strife is like releasing water; therefore stop contention before a quarrel starts.

15 He who justifies the wicked, and he who condemns the just, both of them alike are an abomination to the LORD.

16 Why is there in the hand of a fool the purchase price of wisdom, since he has no heart for it?

17 A friend loves at all times, and a brother is born for adversity.

18 A man devoid of understanding shakes hands in a pledge, and becomes surety for his friend.

19 He who loves transgression loves strife, and he who exalts his gate seeks destruction.

20 He who has a deceitful heart finds no good, and he who has a perverse tongue falls into evil.

21 He who begets a scoffer does so to his sorrow, and the father of a fool has no joy.

22 A merry heart does good, like medicine, but a broken spirit dries the bones.

23 A wicked man accepts a bribe behind the back to pervert the ways of justice.

24 Wisdom is in the sight of him who has understanding, but the eyes of a fool are on the ends of the earth.

25 A foolish son is a grief to his father, and bitterness to her who bore him.

26 Also, to punish the righteous is not good, nor to strike princes for their uprightness.

27 He who has knowledge spares his words, and a man of understanding is of a calm spirit.

28 Even a fool is counted wise when he holds his peace; when he shuts his lips, he is considered perceptive.

choose Your peace today rather than anything that would bring arguments and strife. I want to have a pure heart and a right spirit. Lord, are there any areas in my heart that aren't pure? Please purify my heart. Am I keeping a right spirit?

Keep me from believing or listening to lies. I determine not to listen to those who are full of revenge. Remove liars from my life.

I choose not to be happy at others' calamity or gloat over their misfortunes. I decide never to make fun of the poor and bring dishonor to You.

Help me today, Lord, to forgive and forget others' mistakes, sins, and offenses. Never let me talk about these actions and bring a division among my friends. I choose to be a person of common sense and wisdom who is open to receive effective correction. I don't want to be rebellious and invite judgment into my life. Keep me from repaying evil for good so destruction will be kept from my family.

I choose never to start strife, because once it starts, it's hard to stop. Keep me, Lord, from justifying wicked things and wicked people. I don't want to take part in condemning the just and true. Keep me from having a deceitful heart that doesn't find any good. Remove from me a perverse tongue that leads to evil. I want to have a cheerful heart, because it helps me like medicine. Keep me from a broken spirit that makes me sick.

Lord, guide me in Your wisdom. I choose to make it my main pursuit. Show me how to use my words sparingly, with a calm spirit. Help me to keep my mouth shut when I'm not knowledgeable about something. By staying silent, I'll be considered perceptive and wise.

1   A man who isolates himself seeks his own desire; he rages against all wise judgment.

2   A fool has no delight in understanding, but in expressing his own heart.

3   When the wicked comes, contempt comes also; and with dishonor comes reproach.

4   The words of a man's mouth are deep waters; the wellspring of wisdom is a flowing brook.

5   It is not good to show partiality to the wicked, or to overthrow the righteous in judgment.

6   A fool's lips enter into contention, and his mouth calls for blows.

7   A fool's mouth is his destruction, and his lips are the snare of his soul.

8   The words of a talebearer are like tasty trifles, and they go down into the inmost body.

9   He who is slothful in his work is a brother to him who is a great destroyer.

10  The name of the LORD is a strong tower; the righteous run to it and are safe.

11  The rich man's wealth is his strong city, and like a high wall in his own esteem.

12  Before destruction the heart of a man is haughty, and before honor is humility.

13 He who answers a matter before he hears it, it is folly and shame to him.

14 The spirit of a man will sustain him in sickness, but who can bear a broken spirit?

15 The heart of the prudent acquires knowledge, and the ear of the wise seeks knowledge.

16 A man's gift makes room for him, and brings him before great men.

17 The first one to plead his cause seems right, until his neighbor comes and examines him.

18 Casting lots causes contentions to cease, and keeps the mighty apart.

19 A brother offended is harder to win than a strong city, and contentions are like the bars of a castle.

20 A man's stomach shall be satisfied from the fruit of his mouth, from the produce of his lips he shall be filled.

21 Death and life are in the power of the tongue, and those who love it will eat its fruit.

22 He who finds a wife finds a good thing, and obtains favor from the LORD.

23 The poor man uses entreaties, but the rich answers roughly.

24 A man who has friends must himself be friendly, but there is a friend who sticks closer than a brother.

# CHAPTER 18
## PRAYER

ord, help me love those around me by sharing Your wisdom and love today. I don't want to be an isolated loner who only wants what I want and demands my own way. If I do that, I will find myself in opposition to every wise idea, thought or decision.

I'll not foolishly reject understanding and only express my own thoughts today. Show me how to have deep wellsprings of wisdom flowing out of my life.

Lord, keep me from favoring wicked people and condemning those who do right today. Keep me from saying wrong words that can trap my soul and destroy me. Help me to understand that sin brings disgrace. Are there any rumors or gossip that I have been spreading or believing? Please keep me from tattling, gossiping, and spreading rumors.

Today, I choose to be diligent in everything I do. I believe that You are a fortress, a strong tower, One whom I can run to and be safe. Help me understand that being humble brings honor, while having a haughty heart and being full of pride brings destruction.

Help me to hold my tongue and refrain from answering anything today before knowing all the facts. Talking too soon will only bring folly and shame to me. I choose to seek and acquire Your knowledge today, always learning and listening. Enable me with a healthy, strong spirit that will sustain me in the middle of adversity. If a conflict arises, help me to be patient with others today by taking the time to hear both sides of any problem. I know that only then will I be able to reach an accurate conclusion.

Keep me from offending other people today, because it is almost impossible to win them back once I do. I know that words can either give life or take it. So help me today, Lord, to say good, positive, uplifting words that bring life.

I thank You today for helping me be (find) a good wife. I understand that I (she) am (is) a good thing, and even bring(s) favor from You into my husband's (my) life.

I choose to be friendly to others so friends will be numerous in my life. And thank You again, Lord, that a real friend like You always sticks closer than a brother.

# CHAPTER 19

1 Better is the poor who walks in his integrity than one who is perverse in his lips, and is a fool.

2 Also it is not good for a soul to be without knowledge, and he sins who hastens with his feet.

3 The foolishness of a man twists his way, and his heart frets against the LORD.

4 Wealth makes many friends, but the poor is separated from his friend.

5 A false witness will not go unpunished, and he who speaks lies will not escape.

6 Many entreat the favor of the nobility, and every man is a friend to one who gives gifts.

7 All the brothers of the poor hate him; how much more do his friends go far from him! He may pursue them with words, yet they abandon him.

8 He who gets wisdom loves his own soul; he who keeps understanding will find good.

9 A false witness will not go unpunished, and he who speaks lies shall perish.

10 Luxury is not fitting for a fool, much less for a servant to rule over princes.

11 The discretion of a man makes him slow to anger, and his glory is to overlook a transgression.

12 The king's wrath is like the roaring of a lion, but his favor is like dew on the grass.

13 A foolish son is the ruin of his father, and the contentions of a wife are a continual dripping.

14 Houses and riches are an inheritance from fathers, but a prudent wife is from the LORD.

15 Laziness casts one into a deep sleep, and an idle person will suffer hunger.

16 He who keeps the commandment keeps his soul, but he who is careless of his ways will die.

17 He who has pity on the poor lends to the LORD, and He will pay back what he has given.

18 Chasten your son while there is hope, and do not set your heart on his destruction.

19 A man of great wrath will suffer punishment; for if you rescue him, you will have to do it again.

20 Listen to counsel and receive instruction, that you may be wise in your latter days.

21 There are many plans in a man's heart, nevertheless the LORD'S counsel—that will stand.

22 What is desired in a man is kindness, and a poor man is better than a liar.

23 The fear of the LORD leads to life, and he who has it will abide in satisfaction; he will not be visited with evil.

24 A lazy man buries his hand in the bowl, and will not so much as bring it to his mouth again.

25 Strike a scoffer, and the simple will become wary; rebuke one who has understanding, and he will discern knowledge.

26 He who mistreats his father and chases away his mother is a son who causes shame and brings reproach.

27 Cease listening to instruction, my son, and you will stray from the words of knowledge.

28 A disreputable witness scorns justice, and the mouth of the wicked devours iniquity.

29 Judgments are prepared for scoffers, and beatings for the backs of fools.

ord, I decide to walk in integrity today. I don't want to foolishly say dishonest things. I want to be good to my soul, so I seek Your knowledge. Let me understand that haste makes waste.

I choose not to be foolish because it causes me to go down the wrong path. Help me always to be honest and avoid the punishment that comes on liars.

Today, I want to show that I love my own soul by acquiring wisdom. Help me to understand Your Word and by doing so find what is good.

Assist me in showing good discretion today by being slow to anger and willing to overlook offenses done against me. I want to be a person who can forgive and forget. Is there anyone I need to forgive today, Lord? If there is, help me to forgive them.

Teach me not to be a negative, nagging person. Help me to be positive and sensible. And, Lord, please remove laziness and idleness from my life. I never want to become careless in my ways and invite my own destruction. I want to lead a diligent and productive life, so please help me to keep Your command-ments today. Thank You for preserving my mind, will and emotions.

Show me if there is someone I can help today. Open my heart to have pity on the poor. I know that as I do, I will be giving to You. And You even pay back what I have given!

Lord, thank You for the opportunity to correct my children today while there is still hope. Keep me from setting my heart on their destruction. Stop me from becoming angry with them and suffering my own punishment as a result.

I thank You that even though I have many plans in my heart, it is Your direction that stands. It is Your purpose that always prevails. Help me today to receive sound advice and good instruction that makes me wise in life. Deliver me from being a skeptic or a fool. I don't want to suffer the punishment of their critical ways.

Lord, I decide to be kind to everyone I know today and I choose not to mistreat my parents. Open me to receive all of Your counsel and instruction so I will live wisely and well. Let me see that the fear of You brings me life and causes me to be satisfied, while keeping me from evil. Help me grow today in Your wisdom and grace.

1   Wine is a mocker, strong drink is a brawler, and whoever is led astray by it is not wise.

2   The wrath of a king is like the roaring of a lion; whoever provokes him to anger sins against his own life.

3   It is honorable for a man to stop striving, since any fool can start a quarrel.

4   The lazy man will not plow because of winter; he will beg during harvest and have nothing.

5   Counsel in the heart of man is like deep water, but a man of understanding will draw it out.

6   Most men will proclaim each his own goodness, but who can find a faithful man?

7   The righteous man walks in his integrity; his children are blessed after him.

8   A king who sits on the throne of judgment scatters all evil with his eyes.

9   Who can say, "I have made my heart clean, I am pure from my sin"?

10  Diverse weights and diverse measures, they are both alike, an abomination to the LORD.

11  Even a child is known by his deeds, whether what he does is pure and right.

12  The hearing ear and the seeing eye, the LORD has made them both.

13  Do not love sleep, lest you come to poverty; open your eyes, and you will be satisfied with bread.

14  "It is good for nothing," cries the buyer; but when he has gone his way, then he boasts.

15 There is gold and a multitude of rubies, but the lips of knowledge are a precious jewel.

16 Take the garment of one who is surety for a stranger, and hold it as a pledge when it is for a seductress.

17 Bread gained by deceit is sweet to a man, but afterward his mouth will be filled with gravel.

18 Plans are established by counsel; by wise counsel wage war.

19 He who goes about as a talebearer reveals secrets; therefore do not associate with one who flatters with his lips.

20 Whoever curses his father or his mother, his lamp will be put out in deep darkness.

21 An inheritance gained hastily at the beginning will not be blessed at the end.

22 Do not say, "I will recompense evil"; wait for the LORD, and He will save you.

23 Diverse weights are an abomination to the LORD, and dishonest scales are not good.

24 A man's steps are of the LORD; how then can a man understand his own way?

25 It is a snare for a man to devote rashly something as holy, and afterward to reconsider his vows.

26 A wise king sifts out the wicked, and brings the threshing wheel over them.

27 The spirit of a man is the lamp of the LORD, searching all the inner depths of his heart.

28 Mercy and truth preserve the king, and by lovingkindness he upholds his throne.

29 The glory of young men is their strength, and the splendor of old men is their gray head.

30 Blows that hurt cleanse away evil, as do stripes the inner depths of the heart.

# CHAPTER 20
## PRAYER

hank You, Lord, for keeping me from being led astray by alcohol and for guarding me from quarrels and fighting. Both are foolish activities and I'm grateful for Your presence that gives me strength to resist what is wrong.

I won't make excuses today for not completing my work on time, because when I eliminate alibis from my life, I receive a harvest.

Help me not to proclaim my own goodness today. Give me an opportunity to be a faithful friend. I ask You to help me be a righteous person who walks in integrity. As a result, my children will be blessed.

Lord, I know that I can never make my own heart clean and purify myself from sin. Only You can do that, so I ask You to forgive me of my sins and purify my heart today. Keep me from any area of deceit because it is an abomination to You. Help me understand that everyone, even a child, is known by the good or the evil they do. I decide not to love sleep too much; instead, I will energetically work and see fruitful results.

Lord, keep me from dishonesty and deception today. Thank You for showing me that any apparent sweetness of this strategy always results in a feeling as satisfying as a mouth filled with gravel.

Lead me to form my plans by seeking wise counsel and help me to carry out this advice by getting as much help as I possibly can. What plans do I have that I need to seek wise counsel for today, Lord? Is there anyone I should or shouldn't talk to about these plans? Please show me.

Lord, please help me to stay clear of gossips and flatterers today. Show me who these people are and keep me away from them. Also, help me to understand that quick gain at the start will not necessarily be blessed at the end. Help me to be patient and to trust Your timing.

Today, I choose not to try to get even with others. Instead, I will trust in You and believe that You will justify and save me. Help me not to be deceitful, conniving, or untruthful in any relationship I have.

I trust You today to direct my steps. Help me avoid the trap of making quick, rash commitments and promises, because later I may want to change my mind and not be able to get out of them. Give me clear understanding on how my spirit is like a lamp that You use to examine my innermost being. Help me to see how good correction can eradicate evil from my heart and life.

1 The king's heart is in the hand of the LORD, like the rivers of water; he turns it wherever He wishes.

2 Every way of a man is right in his own eyes, but the LORD weighs the hearts.

3 To do righteousness and justice is more acceptable to the LORD than sacrifice.

4 A haughty look, a proud heart, and the plowing of the wicked are sin.

5 The plans of the diligent lead surely to plenty, but those of everyone who is hasty, surely to poverty.

6 Getting treasures by a lying tongue is the fleeting fantasy of those who seek death.

7 The violence of the wicked will destroy them, because they refuse to do justice.

8 The way of a guilty man is perverse; but as for the pure, his work is right.

9 Better to dwell in a corner of a housetop, than in a house shared with a contentious woman.

10 The soul of the wicked desires evil; his neighbor finds no favor in his eyes.

11 When the scoffer is punished, the simple is made wise; but when the wise is instructed, he receives knowledge.

12 The righteous God wisely considers the house of the wicked, overthrowing the wicked for their wickedness.

13 Whoever shuts his ears to the cry of the poor will also cry him self and not be heard.

14 A gift in secret pacifies anger, and a bribe behind the back, strong wrath.

15 It is a joy for the just to do justice, but destruction will come to the workers of iniquity.

16 A man who wanders from the way of understanding will rest in the assembly of the dead.

17 He who loves pleasure will be a poor man; he who loves wine and oil will not be rich.

18 The wicked shall be a ransom for the righteous, and the unfaithful for the upright.

19 Better to dwell in the wilderness, than with a contentious and angry woman.

20 There is desirable treasure, and oil in the dwelling of the wise, but a foolish man squanders it.

21 He who follows righteousness and mercy finds life, righteousness and honor.

22 A wise man scales the city of the mighty, and brings down the trusted stronghold.

23 Whoever guards his mouth and tongue keeps his soul from troubles.

24 A proud and haughty man—"Scoffer" is his name; he acts with arrogant pride.

25 The desire of the lazy man kills him, for his hands refuse to labor.

26 He covets greedily all day long, but the righteous gives and does not spare.

27 The sacrifice of the wicked is an abomination; how much more when he brings it with wicked intent!

28 A false witness shall perish, but the man who hears him will speak endlessly.

29 A wicked man hardens his face, but as for the upright, he establishes his way.

30 There is no wisdom or understanding or counsel against the LORD.

31 The horse is prepared for the day of battle, but deliverance is of the LORD.

ord, it's good to know that a leader's heart is like a river of water in Your hands that You can turn wherever You wish.

Keep me from justifying every move I make, trying to look right in my own eyes today. I know You examine my heart and weigh my motives. I choose to be directed by You. I determine to do what is right with fairness. Keep me from having an arrogant look and a proud heart. I want to be diligent in everything that I do, causing abundance to come into my life.

Because a hasty lifestyle leads to poverty, help me today, Lord, to fully consider my decisions and pace of life. I choose not to give in to the temptation of dishonest gain because that kind of increase will never last. I decide to be fair and just to those around me today.

Lord, remove any perverse ways from me. Instead, help me always do what's right with pure motives. Help me not to be a contentious, nagging person.

Open my ears to the cry and needs of the poor today, Lord. I know that those who disregard the poor will be ignored in their own time of need.

Help me understand how the love of too much pleasure and alcohol is unwise and leads to poverty. Lord, help me work hard and not try to get something for nothing. Help me follow righteousness and mercy in order to find life, righteousness and honor. Keep me focused and never let me wander from the way of understanding.

Help me not to long for what others have. Instead, I choose to do what is right and to be a liberal giver to others. Do I desire what someone else has today, Lord? Am I envious? If so, please show me.

I realize that no one ever ends up believing a liar, so I determine always to speak honestly. I choose to guard what I say, so I can keep my soul from trouble.

# CHAPTER 22

1 A good name is to be chosen rather than great riches, loving favor rather than silver and gold.

2 The rich and the poor have this in common, the LORD is the maker of them all.

3 A prudent man foresees evil and hides himself, but the simple pass on and are punished.

4 By humility and the fear of the LORD are riches and honor and life.

5 Thorns and snares are in the way of the perverse; he who guards his soul will be far from them.

6 Train up a child in the way he should go, and when he is old he will not depart from it.

7 The rich rules over the poor, and the borrower is servant to the lender.

8 He who sows iniquity will reap sorrow, and the rod of his anger will fail.

9 He who has a generous eye will be blessed, for he gives of his bread to the poor.

10 Cast out the scoffer, and contention will leave; yes, strife and reproach will cease.

11 He who loves purity of heart and has grace on his lips, the king will be his friend.

12 The eyes of the LORD preserve knowledge, but He overthrows the words of the faithless.

13 The lazy man says, "There is a lion outside! I shall be slain in the streets!"

14 The mouth of an immoral woman is a deep pit; he who is abhorred by the LORD will fall there.

15 Foolishness is bound up in the heart of a child; the rod of correction will drive it far from him.

16 He who oppresses the poor to increase his riches, and he who gives to the rich, will surely come to poverty.

17 Incline your ear and hear the words of the wise, and apply your heart to my knowledge;

18 For it is a pleasant thing if you keep them within you; let them all be fixed upon your lips,

19 So that your trust may be in the LORD; I have instructed you today, even you.

20 Have I not written to you excellent things of counsels and knowledge,

21 That I may make you know the certainty of the words of truth, that you may answer words of truth to those who send to you?

22 Do not rob the poor because he is poor, nor oppress the afflicted at the gate;

23 For the LORD will plead their cause, and plunder the soul of those who plunder them.

24 Make no friendship with an angry man, and with a furious man do not go,

25 Lest you learn his ways and set a snare for your soul.

26 Do not be one of those who shakes hands in a pledge, one of those who is surety for debts;

27 If you have nothing with which to pay, why should he take away your bed from under you?

28 Do not remove the ancient landmark which your fathers have set.

29 Do you see a man who excels in his work? He will stand before kings; he will not stand before unknown men.

ord, I choose to have a good name today by displaying outstanding character. A good name is more valuable than great riches, and I want to honor You. I ask You to help me be humble and fear You today because when I do it brings riches, honor and life to me. Help me to foresee evil and stay away from it.

Thank You that right action keeps punishment from my life. Deliver me from the trap of sinful things by guarding my soul from them.

Lord, help me to direct, lead and train my children today in the right way to go. When I do, as they grow older they'll continue to serve You. Is there any way I can lead and train my children better? Please show me. Give me a loving understanding of how the rod of punishment will drive foolishness and folly from them.

Today, help me to be honest, and as a result, You'll keep sorrow and destruction away from me. Keep me from anger that brings failure with it. Help me to show generosity to the poor and in return receive Your blessing. Remove troublemakers, skeptics and critics from me. When they are gone from my life, strife, confusion and contention leave me alone.

I will guard my mind, will and emotions today. Lord, help me to be pure-hearted and to speak words of grace. As I do, leaders will become my friends. Lord, You guard knowledge and have nothing to do with dishonesty. Remove from my life any excuse that keeps me from doing the work I know I'm supposed to do.

Keep me away from immoral people today. I understand that the words of an evil person are like a deep pit that people fall into.

I determine never to oppress the poor in order to increase my own wealth. I refuse to give to the rich in order to gain their favor, because it only brings poverty.

Lord, I know that it's a pleasant thing to keep Your knowledge and wisdom inside me so I open my ears today to hear Your words of wisdom. I choose to diligently seek godly knowledge and to speak words full of wisdom. Doing this helps me to keep my trust in You.

I will never take advantage of or exploit the poor simply because they're poor. Show me how to help those who are afflicted and needy. I know You plead their case and come against the souls of those who take advantage of them. Help me be sensitive today to those with great need.

Lord, keep me away from angry people today. I don't want to become like them and set a snare for my soul. Help me to avoid making any pledges with others today that could entangle me in their debts. I commit to be excellent, skillful and hard-working at whatever I do today. By doing that, success and promotion will come to me and I will find myself associating with great people.

# CHAPTER 23

1 When you sit down to eat with a ruler, consider carefully what is before you;

2 And put a knife to your throat if you are a man given to appetite.

3 Do not desire his delicacies, for they are deceptive food.

4 Do not overwork to be rich; because of your own understanding, cease!

5 Will you set your eyes on that which is not? For riches certainly make themselves wings; they fly away like an eagle toward heaven.

6 Do not eat the bread of a miser, nor desire his delicacies;

7 For as he thinks in his heart, so is he. "Eat and drink!" he says to you, but his heart is not with you.

8 The morsel you have eaten, you will vomit up, and waste your pleasant words.

9 Do not speak in the hearing of a fool, for he will despise the wisdom of your words.

10 Do not remove the ancient landmark, nor enter the fields of the fatherless;

11 For their Redeemer is mighty; he will plead their cause against you.

12 Apply your heart to instruction, and your ears to words of knowledge.

13 Do not withhold correction from a child, for if you beat him with a rod, he will not die.

14 You shall beat him with a rod, and deliver his soul from hell.

15 My son, if your heart is wise, my heart will rejoice—indeed, I myself;

16 Yes, my inmost being will rejoice when your lips speak right things.

17 Do not let your heart envy sinners, but be zealous for the fear of the LORD all the day;

18 For surely there is a hereafter, and your hope will not be cut off.

19 Hear, my son, and be wise; and guide your heart in the way.

20 Do not mix with winebibbers, or with gluttonous eaters of meat;

21 For the drunkard and the glutton will come to poverty, and drowsiness will clothe a man with rags.

22 Listen to your father who begot you, and do not despise your mother when she is old.

23 Buy the truth, and do not sell it, also wisdom and instruction and understanding.

24 The father of the righteous will greatly rejoice, and he who begets a wise child will delight in him.

25 Let your father and your mother be glad, and let her who bore you rejoice.

26 My son, give me your heart, and let your eyes observe my ways.

27 For a harlot is a deep pit, and a seductress is a narrow well.

28 She also lies in wait as for a victim, and increases the unfaithful among men.

29 Who has woe? Who has sorrow? Who has contentions? Who has complaints? Who has wounds without cause? Who has redness of eyes?

30 Those who linger long at the wine, those who go in search of mixed wine.

31 Do not look on the wine when it is red, when it sparkles in the cup, when it swirls around smoothly;

32 At the last it bites like a serpent, and stings like a viper.

33 Your eyes will see strange things, and your heart will utter perverse things.

34 Yes, you will be like one who lies down in the midst of the sea, or like one who lies at the top of the mast, saying:

35 "They have struck me, but I was not hurt; they have beaten me, but I did not feel it. When shall I awake, that I may seek another drink?"

ord, when I have the opportunity to eat with an influential person, let me consider who and what is before me. Help me exhibit good table manners and control over my appetite. I choose not to desire what they have in their life, because I know what they appear to have is not exactly as it seems.

Today, I'll no longer depend on my own wisdom. Instead, I choose Your wisdom and determine to show restraint. I will avoid the empty activity of making money for money's sake. Riches are only temporary; they can disappear in the blink of an eye.

Keep me from associating with miserly, stingy people. They often have ulterior motives in their hearts and talking with them is just a waste of time. Keep me from throwing my words away by speaking to fools, because they won't respect what I have to say. Thank You, Lord, for defending and protecting orphans. Show me how I can help them.

Open my heart and mind to instruction and correction. Are there some areas You want me to have further instruction in today, Lord? What corrections do You have for me? Fine-tune my ears today to Your words of knowledge.

Today, I pray to have a wise heart and to speak the right things. If my children need correction, remind me of Your love so I do it properly, rescuing their souls from hell. I never want to become envious of sinners. Instead, I'll be zealous about my reverence for You. Because of You, I have a wonderful hope and future.

Lord, help me to listen to You and be wise, keeping my heart on the right path. Keep me away from people who drink too much alcohol and are gluttons. They end up in poverty and I don't want to end up there with them.

Today, I won't be lazy. I will listen to my father and respect my mother. I will gain Your truth at any cost and never let go of it. I want to grab onto discernment, wisdom, instruction and understanding.

Keep my heart and eyes pure. Remove all the immoral people who lie in wait for me. I know that relationships with them only bring sorrow, anguish, contention, and injuries into my life. Thank You for keeping me away from the influence of alcohol. It only hurts the drinker by making his mind unsteady and perverting his perspective on life. Why would I want to live like that?

Wonderful Counselor, thank You for hearing my prayer today. I praise You for Your wisdom. Thank You for giving it to me.

# C H A P T E R 24

1 Do not be envious of evil men, nor desire to be with them;
2 For their heart devises violence, and their lips talk of trouble-making.
3 Through wisdom a house is built, and by understanding it is established;
4 By knowledge the rooms are filled with all precious and pleasant riches.
5 A wise man is strong, yes, a man of knowledge increases strength;
6 For by wise counsel you will wage your own war, and in a multitude of counselors there is safety.
7 Wisdom is too lofty for a fool; he does not open his mouth in the gate.
8 He who plots to do evil will be called a schemer.
9 The devising of foolishness is sin, and the scoffer is an abomination to men.
10 If you faint in the day of adversity, your strength is small.
11 Deliver those who are drawn toward death, and hold back those stumbling to the slaughter.
12 If you say, "Surely we did not know this," does not He who weighs the hearts consider it? He who keeps your soul, does He not know it? And will He not render to each man according to his deeds?
13 My son, eat honey because it is good, and the honeycomb which is sweet to your taste;
14 So shall the knowledge of wisdom be to your soul; if you have found it, there is a prospect, and your hope will not be cut off.
15 Do not lie in wait, O wicked man, against the dwelling of the righteous; do not plunder his resting place;
16 For a righteous man may fall seven times and rise again, but the wicked shall fall by calamity.

17 Do not rejoice when your enemy falls, and do not let your heart be glad when he stumbles;

18 Lest the LORD see it, and it displease Him, and He turn away His wrath from him.

19 Do not fret because of evildoers, nor be envious of the wicked;

20 For there will be no prospect for the evil man; the lamp of the wicked will be put out.

21 My son, fear the LORD and the king; do not associate with those given to change;

22 For their calamity will rise suddenly, and who knows the ruin those two can bring?

23 These things also belong to the wise: it is not good to show partiality in judgment.

24 He who says to the wicked, "You are righteous," him the people will curse; nations will abhor him.

25 But those who rebuke the wicked will have delight, and a good blessing will come upon them.

26 He who gives a right answer kisses the lips.

27 Prepare your outside work, make it fit for yourself in the field; and afterward build your house.

28 Do not be a witness against your neighbor without cause, for would you deceive with your lips?

29 Do not say, "I will do to him just as he has done to me; I will render to the man according to his work."

30 I went by the field of the lazy man, and by the vineyard of the man devoid of understanding;

31 And there it was, all overgrown with thorns; its surface was covered with nettles; its stone wall was broken down.

32 When I saw it, I considered it well; I looked on it and received instruction:

33 A little sleep, a little slumber, a little folding of the hands to rest;

34 So shall your poverty come like a prowler, and your need like an armed man.

# CHAPTER 24
## PRAYER

ord, keep me from becoming jealous of ungodly people today. Remove from me any desire to be with them or like them. Their hearts plot evil schemes and destruction. Their words are full of trouble. Are there people like that who are influencing my life? Lord, please show me who they are so I can discontinue my relationship with them.

Lord, today I see that it takes wisdom to build anything. I understand that by acquiring understanding, a right foundation for long-term growth is established. I see that by acquiring knowledge, overflowing abundance comes to me. Help me see that Your wisdom brings increasing strength and knowledge.

I promise to seek advice when conflicts with others arise. Thank You for safety that comes to me from listening to many good advisors. Remove foolishness and help me not to be critical or make fun of others.

Strengthen me so I don't give up in times of trouble. Help me to rescue those who are on the path of death and are moving blindly towards destruction. You know and weigh the motives of every person's heart. You know mine, and You will reward everyone according to his deeds.

Your wisdom is like honey; it's so sweet to my soul. It assures me of a good future and that You will never abandon me.

If a righteous person falls down many times, he rises again and again. When the wicked are brought down by calamity and when my enemy falls or stumbles, help me not to be thrilled, Lord. If you see me having that attitude, You will disapprove, and it will disrupt Your due course of judgment. Only You are worthy to avenge wrongdoers.

I don't care about the temporal success of wicked people, because I know they have no future. The path they're on is a dead-end street, going the wrong way fast. Instead, I choose to fear, love and reverence You, Lord.

Help me choose right relationships. Give me Your wisdom to stay free from wrong associations with rebellious people, and deliver me from their evil plans. Help me avoid the calamity and disaster that comes through relationship with them.

Lord, help me to see injustice today. Don't let me call the wicked "good." Rather, give me the courage to expose the wicked for who they are. As a result, I will see blessings come into my life.

As long as I live, I have decided that an honest answer will always be my response. Keep me from speaking against my neighbor without cause or using my lips to deceive. I won't try to get even with anyone.

I don't want to live a life that is empty of understanding today. Help me understand the lesson I can learn from the life of a lazy person. All around the lazy, things go unattended and fall apart. Poverty comes on them like a thief, and their needs go unmet. Today, I decide to live a diligent life.

# CHAPTER 25

1 These also are proverbs of Solomon which the men of Hezekiah king of Judah copied:

2 It is the glory of God to conceal a matter, but the glory of kings is to search out a matter.

3 As the heavens for height and the earth for depth, so the heart of kings is unsearchable.

4 Take away the dross from silver, and it will go to the silversmith for jewelry.

5 Take away the wicked from before the king, and his throne will be established in righteousness.

6 Do not exalt yourself in the presence of the king, and do not stand in the place of the great;

7 For it is better that he say to you, "Come up here," than that you should be put lower in the presence of the prince, whom your eyes have seen.

8 Do not go hastily to court; for what will you do in the end, when your neighbor has put you to shame?

9 Debate your case with your neighbor, and do not disclose the secret to another;

10 Lest he who hears it expose your shame, and your reputation be ruined.

11 A word fitly spoken is like apples of gold in settings of silver.

12 Like an earring of gold and an ornament of fine gold is a wise rebuker to an obedient ear.

13 Like the cold of snow in time of harvest is a faithful messenger to those who send him, for he refreshes the soul of his masters.

14 Whoever falsely boasts of giving is like clouds and wind without rain.

15 By long forbearance a ruler is persuaded, and a gentle tongue breaks a bone.

16 Have you found honey? Eat only as much as you need, lest you be filled with it and vomit.

17 Seldom set foot in your neighbor's house, lest he become weary of you and hate you.

18 A man who bears false witness against his neighbor is like a club, a sword, and a sharp arrow.

19 Confidence in an unfaithful man in time of trouble is like a bad tooth and a foot out of joint.

20 Like one who takes away a garment in cold weather, and like vinegar on soda, is one who sings songs to a heavy heart.

21 If your enemy is hungry, give him bread to eat; and if he is thirsty, give him water to drink;

22 For so you will heap coals of fire on his head, and the LORD will reward you.

23 The north wind brings forth rain, and a backbiting tongue an angry countenance.

24 It is better to dwell in a corner of a housetop, than in a house shared with a contentious woman.

25 As cold water to a weary soul, so is good news from a far country.

26 A righteous man who falters before the wicked is like a murky spring and a polluted well.

27 It is not good to eat much honey; so to seek one's own glory is not glory.

28 Whoever has no rule over his own spirit is like a city broken down, without walls.

ord, I see today that it is Your glory and privilege to keep things to Yourself, but that it is the glory of leaders to search out things and discover them. I also understand that it is better to be invited to a place of honor than to be humiliated by trying to exalt myself. So, Lord, please help me to know my place today and be content where You have placed me.

Because I choose to be wise today, I won't be in a rush to bring others to court. It is always possible that there may be a good explanation for wrongs that occur. Therefore, I will discuss any conflict privately to avoid humiliation. Don't let me betray another person's confidence, because the one who hears it may expose my shame and damage my reputation. Help me to understand that an evil, gossiping tongue always brings an angry response from others.

Lord, help me speak the right word at the best time. A right word is as valuable as fine jewelry. Is there a good word I can share with someone else today? Help me be a faithful friend who refreshes others. Please help me have a gentle tongue. Keep me from the emptiness of falsely boasting about what I give today.

I choose to be fair to my friends and neighbors. I want to be sensitive about the number of times I visit with them so I don't overstay my welcome. Keep me from lying about my neighbors. Open my eyes to see if I'm putting confidence in an unfaithful friend because doing this is like chewing on a sore tooth or trying to run on a dislocated foot.

Help me today to be sensitive to anyone I encounter with a heavy heart. I don't want to hurt them more than they already are by trying to cheer them up in the wrong way.

I choose to follow Your advice concerning enemies today; that is, if they need something, I'll give it to them if I can. I know that when I do, You will be their judge and reward me for it.

Keep me from contentious people today, Lord. I don't want to be a polluted person, so give me the strength to oppose the wicked. Keep me from the emptiness of promoting myself. I want to be a person of self-control, Lord, so help me be strong in You.

# CHAPTER 26

1 As snow in summer and rain in harvest, so honor is not fitting for a fool.

2 Like a flitting sparrow, like a flying swallow, so a curse without cause shall not alight.

3 A whip for the horse, a bridle for the donkey, and a rod for the fool's back.

4 Do not answer a fool according to his folly, lest you also be like him.

5 Answer a fool according to his folly, lest he be wise in his own eyes.

6 He who sends a message by the hand of a fool cuts off his own feet and drinks violence.

7 Like the legs of the lame that hang limp is a proverb in the mouth of fools.

8 Like one who binds a stone in a sling is he who gives honor to a fool.

9 Like a thorn that goes into the hand of a drunkard is a proverb in the mouth of fools.

10 The great God who formed everything gives the fool his hire and the transgressor his wages.

11 As a dog returns to his own vomit, so a fool repeats his folly.

12 Do you see a man wise in his own eyes? There is more hope for a fool than for him.

13 The lazy man says, "There is a lion in the road! A fierce lion is in the streets!"

14 As a door turns on its hinges, so does the lazy man on his bed.

15 The lazy man buries his hand in the bowl; it wearies him to bring it back to his mouth.

16 The lazy man is wiser in his own eyes than seven men who can answer sensibly.

17 He who passes by and meddles in a quarrel not his own is like one who takes a dog by the ears.

18 Like a madman who throws firebrands, arrows, and death,

19 Is the man who deceives his neighbor, and says, "I was only joking!"

20 Where there is no wood, the fire goes out; and where there is no talebearer, strife ceases.

21 As charcoal is to burning coals, and wood to fire, so is a contentious man to kindle strife.

22 The words of a talebearer are like tasty trifles, and they go down into the inmost body.

23 Fervent lips with a wicked heart are like earthenware covered with silver dross.

24 He who hates, disguises it with his lips, and lays up deceit within himself;

25 When he speaks kindly, do not believe him, for there are seven abominations in his heart;

26 Though his hatred is covered by deceit, his wickedness will be revealed before the assembly.

27 Whoever digs a pit will fall into it, and he who rolls a stone will have it roll back on him.

28 A lying tongue hates those who are crushed by it, and a flattering mouth works ruin.

hank You for showing me today that there is no honor in being a fool. When responding to someone who is foolish, I don't want to act like them, because when I do, I become like them. Help me to avoid hiring anyone who is foolish or rebellious. I understand that a fool always repeats his mistake, which is as pathetic as a dog returning to its own vomit.

It's dumb for me to be wise in my own eyes. In fact, there is more hope for a fool than for me when I do that. Please show me today any areas where I think I don't need Your wisdom.

I'm not going to be lazy today, Lord. Convict me for any dumb excuses I have for missed deadlines or laziness on my job. Remove every alibi and excuse from my life.

Today, I'm going to pass by and avoid the quarrels of others. Thank You for showing me that the benefit of meddling in the fights of others is about as fun as grabbing a cat by the tail or a dog by the ears.

Keep me from deceiving my neighbors today, even if it's only jokingly. I want to help end strife today by never being a talebearer or participating in gossip. I can discourage strife by being a peaceful person. Even though others may want to hear what I know, I'm going to keep gossip to myself. Please close my lips if a touchy subject comes up. Keep me from speaking passionately about things for which I have an ungodly ulterior motive. Let my words be full of truth today.

Lord, help me recognize those around me who may be full of hatred today. Let me see through their deceptive words. Help me to recognize that people who harbor evil in their heart are full of deceit. When they speak words that seem to be good and truthful, help me to see through their deception. You've shown me that seven different abominations fill their heart, and that their deceitful wickedness will eventually be exposed in front of many people. Please deliver me from their plots so I won't fall into their pit.

# CHA27TER

1 Do not boast about tomorrow, for you do not know what a day may bring forth.

2 Let another man praise you, and not your own mouth; a stranger, and not your own lips.

3 A stone is heavy and sand is weighty, but a fool's wrath is heavier than both of them.

4 Wrath is cruel and anger a torrent, but who is able to stand before jealousy?

5 Open rebuke is better than love carefully concealed.

6 Faithful are the wounds of a friend, but the kisses of an enemy are deceitful.

7 A satisfied soul loathes the honeycomb, but to a hungry soul every bitter thing is sweet.

8 Like a bird that wanders from its nest is a man who wanders from his place.

9 Ointment and perfume delight the heart, and the sweetness of a man's friend gives delight by hearty counsel.

10 Do not forsake your own friend or your father's friend, nor go to your brother's house in the day of your calamity; better is a neighbor nearby than a brother far away.

11 My son, be wise, and make my heart glad, that I may answer him who reproaches me.

12 A prudent man foresees evil and hides himself; the simple pass on and are punished.

13 Take the garment of him who is surety for a stranger, and hold it in pledge when he is surety for a seductress.

14 He who blesses his friend with a loud voice, rising early in the morning, it will be counted a curse to him.

15 A continual dripping on a very rainy day and a contentious woman are alike;

16 Whoever restrains her restrains the wind, and grasps oil with his right hand.

17 As iron sharpens iron, so a man sharpens the countenance of his friend.

18 Whoever keeps the fig tree will eat its fruit; so he who waits on his master will be honored.

19 As in water face reflects face, so a man's heart reveals the man.

20 Hell and Destruction are never full; so the eyes of man are never satisfied.

21 The refining pot is for silver and the furnace for gold, and a man is valued by what others say of him.

22 Though you grind a fool in a mortar with a pestle along with crushed grain, yet his foolishness will not depart from him.

23 Be diligent to know the state of your flocks, and attend to your herds;

24 For riches are not forever, nor does a crown endure to all generations.

25 When the hay is removed, and the tender grass shows itself, and the herbs of the mountains are gathered in,

26 The lambs will provide your clothing, and the goats the price of a field;

27 You shall have enough goats' milk for your food, for the food of your household, and the nourishment of your maid-servants.

# CHAPTER 27
## PRAYER

ear Lord, is it really possible for me to know what tomorrow will bring? Of course not. But I know You know, so I will trust in You.

If I am to receive any praise today, let it come from someone else and not me. Keep me from being jealous of others because jealousy can be more dangerous and explosive than anger.

Help me to see that what a true friend does is more trustworthy than anything an enemy says. And when a friend corrects me, it's more valuable than love that's never expressed.

Bring focus to me so I can stay on the right path. I don't want to be a person who won't settle down. Send people into my life who can give me timely advice that refreshes my soul. Help me never to abandon or forsake my own friends or a friend of the family. Thank You for all of them, because if problems come my way, it's better to have a close friend than a brother who's far away.

Help me to be wise and bring joy to the heart of my parents today. Keep me from being ignorant, walking blindly and suffering as a result of it. Help me to be prudent and foresee impending danger so I can stay away from it.

Stop me from being a quarrelsome person who wearies others like the continuous dripping on a rainy day. Let my relationships be like iron sharpening iron so that we both bring out the best in each other.

Help me to always honor my boss at work. In doing so, I know You will reward me. As water reflects my face, so my heart reflects me. Create in me a pure heart, Lord.

Help me to see that each of us is tested by the praise we receive. So, Lord, today, I will keep my eyes and ears towards You.

Keep me from being a fool and living a foolish life because they go hand in hand. I choose to be diligent with everything that I'm responsible for and to watch every interest closely. Do I have some "blind spots" regarding my interests and responsibilities, Lord? Help me to be diligent with what I have right now because neither riches nor positions inherited from generations past last forever.

1   The wicked flee when no one pursues, but the righteous are bold as a lion.

2   Because of the transgression of a land, many are its princes; but by a man of understanding and knowledge right will be prolonged.

3   A poor man who oppresses the poor is like a driving rain which leaves no food.

4   Those who forsake the law praise the wicked, but such as keep the law contend with them.

5   Evil men do not understand justice, but those who seek the LORD understand all.

6   Better is the poor who walks in his integrity than one perverse in his ways, though he be rich.

7   Whoever keeps the law is a discerning son, but a companion of gluttons shames his father.

8   One who increases his possessions by usury and extortion gathers it for him who will pity the poor.

9   One who turns away his ear from hearing the law, even his prayer is an abomination.

10  Whoever causes the upright to go astray in an evil way, he himself will fall into his own pit; but the blameless will inherit good.

11  The rich man is wise in his own eyes, but the poor who has understanding searches him out.

12  When the righteous rejoice, there is great glory; but when the wicked arise, men hide themselves.

13  He who covers his sins will not prosper, but whoever confesses and forsakes them will have mercy.

14 Happy is the man who is always reverent, but he who hardens his heart will fall into calamity.

15 Like a roaring lion and a charging bear is a wicked ruler over poor people.

16 A ruler who lacks understanding is a great oppressor, but he who hates covetousness will prolong his days.

17 A man burdened with bloodshed will flee into a pit; let no one help him.

18 Whoever walks blamelessly will be saved, but he who is perverse in his ways will suddenly fall.

19 He who tills his land will have plenty of bread, but he who follows frivolity will have poverty enough!

20 A faithful man will abound with blessings, but he who hastens to be rich will not go unpunished.

21 To show partiality is not good, because for a piece of bread a man will transgress.

22 A man with an evil eye hastens after riches, and does not consider that poverty will come upon him.

23 He who rebukes a man will find more favor afterward than he who flatters with the tongue.

24 Whoever robs his father or his mother, and says, "It is no transgression," the same is companion to a destroyer.

25 He who is of a proud heart stirs up strife, but he who trusts in the LORD will be prospered.

26 He who trusts in his own heart is a fool, but whoever walks wisely will be delivered.

27 He who gives to the poor will not lack, but he who hides his eyes will have many curses.

28 When the wicked arise, men hide themselves; but when they perish, the righteous increase.

# CHAPTER 28
## PRAYER

ord, I see that wicked people spend their lives running from things that aren't after them. But, those who are pure and honest in their dealings can always be as bold as a lion. So teach me, Lord, to be a person of understanding who lives a rock-solid life. Keep me from oppressing the poor in any way. I choose never to turn my back on Your Word or praise the wicked. Instead, I'll follow Your Word and oppose evil people. I will never turn a deaf ear to Your Word, Lord, so my prayers will be pleasing to You.

Lord, let me see today how important it is to have integrity, because it is better to have integrity and be poor than to be evil with great riches. As I seek Your counsel, I want to know what is right. Is there any area of my life today where I lack integrity? Is there anything You want me to change or do differently?

Lord, I commit to follow Your Word and to be a discerning person. Let me see today, Lord, that evil people who make themselves richer by cheating others with excessive interest eventually lose whatever they gained.

Lord, help me to steer good people away from bad choices today. I want to be blameless and receive a good reward from You. As I prosper, help me to avoid becoming wise in my own eyes.

I choose not to cover up my sins today because I won't prosper if I do that. Rather, I confess and abandon them, asking for Your mercy and forgiveness. I will be reverent to You today and as a result, become a happy, blessed person. Remove from me a hard heart; I don't want the calamity and trouble arrogance produces.

Lead me away from wicked leaders who take advantage of others. Lord, please help me never to oppress others that I lead. I choose to hate dishonesty and ill-gotten gain. This decision prolongs my life. Help me to walk blamelessly so I will be kept safe. Deliver me from any perverse ways that could make me fall. I choose to work hard with what's in my hand to do. I won't chase after unimportant things or play around and by doing that, I'll keep poverty out of my life.

Lord, I want to be faithful to You and abound with blessings today. Keep me from trying to get rich quick because that will only make me poor. Help me to treat everyone I know fairly. Let me not hesitate if it's right to correct someone else. As hard as it may seem at the moment, I know I'll find more favor after I help them than if I dishonestly flatter them. Never let me steal from my mother or father and then say that it's not wrong. If I do that, it is like becoming best friends with the devil.

Remove from me a proud heart that stirs up strife today. Remind me of how foolish it is to depend on my own heart. Rather, let me always trust in You and prosper. Send people into my life who are full of wisdom so I will be kept safe. Finally, Lord, send opportunities my way today to give to the poor, then I will lack nothing in my life.

# CHAPTER 29

1   He who is often rebuked, and hardens his neck, will suddenly be destroyed, and that without remedy.

2   When the righteous are in authority, the people rejoice; but when a wicked man rules, the people groan.

3   Whoever loves wisdom makes his father rejoice, but a companion of harlots wastes his wealth.

4   The king establishes the land by justice, but he who receives bribes overthrows it.

5   A man who flatters his neighbor spreads a net for his feet.

6   By transgression an evil man is snared, but the righteous sings and rejoices.

7   The righteous considers the cause of the poor, but the wicked does not understand such knowledge.

8   Scoffers set a city aflame, but wise men turn away wrath.

9   If a wise man contends with a foolish man, whether the fool rages or laughs, there is no peace.

10   The bloodthirsty hate the blameless, but the upright seek his well-being.

11   A fool vents all his feelings, but a wise man holds them back.

12   If a ruler pays attention to lies, all his servants become wicked.

13   The poor man and the oppressor have this in common: the LORD gives light to the eyes of both.

14   The king who judges the poor with truth, his throne will be established forever.

15 The rod and rebuke give wisdom, but a child left to himself brings shame to his mother.

16 When the wicked are multiplied, transgression increases; but the righteous will see their fall.

17 Correct your son, and he will give you rest; yes, he will give delight to your soul.

18 Where there is no revelation, the people cast off restraint; but happy is he who keeps the law.

19 A servant will not be corrected by mere words; for though he understands, he will not respond.

20 Do you see a man hasty in his words? There is more hope for a fool than for him.

21 He who pampers his servant from childhood will have him as a son in the end.

22 An angry man stirs up strife, and a furious man abounds in transgression.

23 A man's pride will bring him low, but the humble in spirit will retain honor.

24 Whoever is a partner with a thief hates his own life; he swears to tell the truth, but reveals nothing.

25 The fear of man brings a snare, but whoever trusts in the LORD shall be safe.

26 Many seek the ruler's favor, but justice for man comes from the LORD.

27 An unjust man is an abomination to the righteous, and he who is upright in the way is an abomination to the wicked.

ord, I want always to be open for opportunities to improve, even if I have to make changes over and over. So I make this quality decision: I choose to remain open to improvement even after numerous constructive criticisms, because I know if I don't, I may be suddenly stopped without getting another chance.

Help me love wisdom every day of my life. By doing so, I will make my father happy and be kept from immoral people who can destroy my life. When I have an opportunity to lead, let me lead honestly while never accepting any kind of bribe from anyone. Keep me from flattering people, because when I do I set a trap for myself. Deliver me from wicked people so I won't be trapped by sin. Instead, I choose to be free by singing, rejoicing, and being righteous.

I want to see and care about the poor today. Change my words and thoughts so I don't become a cynic. I choose to never argue with foolish people; then, I can avoid strife and worthless conflicts.

Lord, give me opportunities today to support and encourage people who walk honorably before You. I will always respect honest people.

Teach me to keep from saying everything I feel. It is wise to keep my mouth shut and hold back what I want to say. Train me to think before I talk so I don't speak in haste. Only hopeless fools do that. As a leader, help me see when someone is lying, because it won't only affect me, but it will also hurt those who work with me.

Never let me ignore my children when they need the rod of correction because it imparts wisdom. Let me know when the rod is needed, realizing that sometimes correction doesn't come by words alone. Help me to be consistent in disciplining my children. I know when I train them they will bring delight to my soul.

Guide me to be a person of vision and revelation. By doing so, I will live a fruitful life. Let Your blessings come to me as I keep Your commandments.

Remove anger from me. It stirs up strife and dissension while causing me to commit many sins. And, Lord, keep me from being full of pride today because it limits my growth. Show me how to be humble and gain Your honor.

Keep me away from any association with people who steal. Am I in any relationships with people who are dishonest? Lord, expose them to me so I can disassociate with them.

I decide today to be free from the fear of others, because this kind of thinking is always an entrapment. Instead, I choose to trust in You and be safe. When I desire justice in my life, I turn to You. Real justice only comes from You.

1   The words of Agur the son of Jakeh, his utterance. This man declared to Ithiel—to Ithiel and Ucal:

2   Surely I am more stupid than any man, and do not have the understanding of a man.

3   I neither learned wisdom nor have knowledge of the Holy One.

4   Who has ascended into heaven, or descended? Who has gathered the wind in His fists? Who has bound the waters in a garment? Who has established all the ends of the earth? What is His name, and what is His Son's name, if you know?

5   Every word of God is pure; he is a shield to those who put their trust in Him.

6   Do not add to His words, lest He rebuke you, and you be found a liar.

7   Two things I request of You (Deprive me not before I die):

8   Remove falsehood and lies far from me; give me neither poverty nor riches—feed me with the food allotted to me;

9   Lest I be full and deny You, and say, "Who is the LORD?" Or lest I be poor and steal, and profane the name of my God.

10  Do not malign a servant to his master, lest he curse you, and you be found guilty.

11  There is a generation that curses its father, and does not bless its mother.

12  There is a generation that is pure in its own eyes, yet is not washed from its filthiness.

13  There is a generation—oh, how lofty are their eyes! And their eyelids are lifted up.

14  There is a generation whose teeth are like swords, and whose fangs are like knives, to devour the poor from off the earth, and the needy from among men.

15  The leech has two daughters—give and Give! There are three things that are never satisfied, four never say, "Enough!":

16 The grave, the barren womb, the earth that is not satisfied with water—and the fire never says, "Enough!"

17 The eye that mocks his father, and scorns obedience to his mother, the ravens of the valley will pick it out, and the young eagles will eat it.

18 There are three things which are too wonderful for me, yes, four which I do not understand:

19 The way of an eagle in the air, the way of a serpent on a rock, the way of a ship in the midst of the sea, and the way of a man with a virgin.

20 This is the way of an adulterous woman: she eats and wipes her mouth, and says, "I have done no wickedness."

21 For three things the earth is perturbed, yes, for four it cannot bear up:

22 For a servant when he reigns, a fool when he is filled with food,

23 A hateful woman when she is married, and a maidservant who succeeds her mistress.

24 There are four things which are little on the earth, but they are exceedingly wise:

25 The ants are a people not strong, yet they prepare their food in the summer;

26 The rock badgers are a feeble folk, yet they make their homes in the crags;

27 The locusts have no king, yet they all advance in ranks;

28 The spider skillfully grasps with its hands, and it is in kings' palaces.

29 There are three things which are majestic in pace, yes, four which are stately in walk:

30 A lion, which is mighty among beasts and does not turn away from any;

31 A greyhound, a male goat also, and a king whose troops are with him.

32 If you have been foolish in exalting yourself, or if you have devised evil, put your hand on your mouth.

33 For as the churning of milk produces butter, and wringing the nose produces blood, so the forcing of wrath produces strife.

# CHAPTER 30
## PRAYER

ord, I humble myself before Your awesome presence today. I know it is You who ascended and descended from heaven, gathered the wind in Your fists, wrapped up the waters in Your garment, and established all the ends of the earth. So thank You again today, Lord, for sharing Your wisdom with me.

Your Word is pure and acts as a shield to me when I put my trust in You. I will never add to Your Word so You won't have to rebuke me and prove me to be a liar.

Today, I ask two things of You. First, take falsehood and lies far away from me. Second, I ask that You meet all my needs as You see fit and help me be content with Your provision. That way, I will never have too much and be tempted to deny You saying, "Who is the Lord?", or have too little and be tempted to steal and dishonor Your name.

Lord, keep me from falsely accusing a person to their employer; I want to avoid a liar's judgment. How have I been treating my parents lately? I promise to never curse my father or forget to bless my mother. What are some ways that I can be better to my parents today?

Keep me from being pure or faultless in my own eyes despite my many sins. I don't want to be a leach to others saying, "Give me, give me," and never be satisfied. Keep me from being haughty and proud. Never let me take advantage of the poor.

Help me to learn wisdom from these four small creatures: the ant, that is not strong, but carefully organizes and plans for the future by storing up food in the summertime; the rock badger, that is a small animal yet protects itself by living within the rocks; the locust, that has no particular leader, yet is effective by working together with the others, advancing orderly in their ranks; and the spider, that is so persevering and industrious it can be found everywhere, even in a king's palace.

Keep me from being foolish by exalting myself or by devising evil. Help me understand that as the churning of milk produces butter and a blow to the nose produces blood, so stirring up anger always causes quarrels. If I am tempted to cause strife today, lead me to be quiet instead, covering my mouth with my hand.

# C H A P T E R 31

1 The words of King Lemuel, the utterance which his mother taught him:

2 What, my son? And what, son of my womb? And what, son of my vows?

3 Do not give your strength to women, nor your ways to that which destroys kings.

4 It is not for kings, O Lemuel, it is not for kings to drink wine, nor for princes intoxicating drink;

5 Lest they drink and forget the law, and pervert the justice of all the afflicted.

6 Give strong drink to him who is perishing, and wine to those who are bitter of heart.

7 Let him drink and forget his poverty, and remember his misery no more.

8 Open your mouth for the speechless, in the cause of all who are appointed to die.

9 Open your mouth, judge righteously, and plead the cause of the poor and needy.

10 Who can find a virtuous wife? For her worth is far above rubies.

11 The heart of her husband safely trusts her; so he will have no lack of gain.

12 She does him good and not evil all the days of her life.

13 She seeks wool and flax, and willingly works with her hands.

14 She is like the merchant ships, she brings her food from afar.

15 She also rises while it is yet night, and provides food for her household, and a portion for her maidservants.

16 She considers a field and buys it; from her profits she plants a vineyard.

17 She girds herself with strength, and strengthens her arms.

18 She perceives that her merchandise is good, and her lamp does not go out by night.

19 She stretches out her hands to the distaff, and her hand holds the spindle.

20 She extends her hand to the poor, yes, she reaches out her hands to the needy.

21 She is not afraid of snow for her household, for all her household is clothed with scarlet.

22 She makes tapestry for herself; her clothing is fine linen and purple.

23 Her husband is known in the gates, when he sits among the elders of the land.

24 She makes linen garments and sells them, and supplies sashes for the merchants.

25 Strength and honor are her clothing; she shall rejoice in time to come.

26 She opens her mouth with wisdom, and on her tongue is the law of kindness.

27 She watches over the ways of her household, and does not eat the bread of idleness.

28 Her children rise up and call her blessed; her husband also, and he praises her:

29 "Many daughters have done well, but you excel them all."

30 Charm is deceitful and beauty is passing, but a woman who fears the LORD, she shall be praised.

31 Give her of the fruit of her hands, and let her own works praise her in the gates.

# CHAPTER 31
## PRAYER

[If a woman, pray this for yourself]:

ord, keep me from being a promiscuous woman who takes away the strength of men and destroys leaders. I don't want to make a fool of myself by drinking alcohol and disqualifying myself from helping those who are oppressed. Instead, help me to defend those who can't help themselves. Help me speak out for justice and stand up for the poor.

Thank You for helping me be a moral woman. And thank You for showing me that virtue is more precious than fine gems. I thank You that my husband's (future husband's) heart can safely trust in me. He has full confidence in me. Show him how to treat me with respect and dignity, and teach me how to be good to him. Is there anything special that I can do today for my husband (future husband)?

Help me get up early so I can prepare for my family every day. I choose to be wise with my purchases using the profits and savings to gain even more. Open my eyes to see the best possible bargains. Give me strength and a willingness to work into the night when a project requires it. Help me to be a diligent, vigorous worker, well able to do whatever tasks I need to perform every day. I want to work skillfully, eagerly, and willingly with my hands.

Help me open my arms to the poor and my hands to the needy. Assist me in thinking ahead to prepare my household for bad weather so that everyone is clothed appropriately.

Lord, help me to understand that by being virtuous I am a positive reflection on my husband. Show me how my actions can bring him respect and favor in our community. Help me to be a person of strength and honor.

And finally, Lord, help me to fearlessly look forward to the future. Fill my mouth with wisdom and my tongue with words of kindness. Lead me to be careful about everything that goes on in my house. I thank You that my children greet me with blessings and even praise me. Help me to see that charm and beauty can be deceitful, but that a woman who fears You will be honored and praised.

# CHAPTER 31
## PRAYER

[If a man, pray this for yourself]:

ord, I ask that You will show me the pitfalls of giving my strength away to evil, promiscuous women who seek to destroy leaders. I thank You for reminding me of the foolishness of drinking alcohol. I want to be a help to the oppressed, and alcohol only clouds my mind. Help me always to defend those who can't help themselves. Help me to speak out for justice and to stand up for the poor.

Thank You, Lord, for giving me Your wisdom that shows me the character of a truly virtuous woman. Thank You for helping me have (find) a virtuous wife. Because of Your wisdom, I understand that her worth is far more valuable than precious gems. As her husband, my heart safely trusts in her. I have full confidence in her and treasure her. I thank You that she is good and not evil to me throughout her life. Help her work skillfully, eagerly and willingly with her hands, meeting the needs of our family. Is there anything special I can do for my wife (future wife) today? Please show me, Lord.

I pray that my virtuous wife (future wife) is wise with her purchases and uses the profits and savings to produce even more. I also thank You that she is a diligent and vigorous worker, and that she is well able to do whatever tasks she needs to perform. Help her to be on the look-out for the best possible bargains. Thank You that she opens her arms to the poor and reaches out her hands to the needy. I'm thankful that she thinks ahead and prepares our entire household for bad weather by seeing that everyone is clothed appropriately.

Because she is such a virtuous woman, I have respect and favor in my community. Thank You that because my wife (future wife) is a person of strength and honor, she stands out like a beautiful dress. Thank You that she is not afraid of the future, and that she confidently looks forward to it. It is wonderful to hear her wisdom and relax in her beautiful kindness.

I thank You that my wife (future wife) is careful about everything that goes on throughout our house and that she is not a lazy person. Our children call her blessed, and I praise her saying, "Many other women have done good things, but You surpass them all. You are the best one!"

Help me to see that charm is deceitful and beauty doesn't last, but a woman who fears God will be praised. Show me how to reward her often for what she has done. Let others praise my excellent wife for her godly example.

# PROVERBS PRINCIPLES FOR:

## ACHIEVEMENT
Through wisdom a house is built, and by
understanding it is established.
Prov. 24:3

## ADVICE
Where there is no counsel, the people fall; but
in the multitude of counselors there is safety.
Prov. 11:14

## ANGER
He who is slow to anger is better than the
mighty, and he who rules his spirit than he
who takes a city.
Prov. 16:32

## CHARACTER
He who walks with integrity walks securely, but
he who perverts his ways will become known.
Prov. 10:9

## COMPASSION
He who oppresses the poor reproaches his
Maker, but he who honors Him has mercy on
the needy.
Prov. 14:31

## CONCEIT

Do you see a man wise in his own eyes? There is more hope for a fool than for him.
Prov. 26:12

## DILIGENCE

Go to the ant, you sluggard! Consider her ways and be wise.
Prov. 6:6

## DIRECTION

A man's heart plans his ways, but the LORD directs his steps.
Prov. 16:9

## DISCIPLINE

He who disdains instruction despises his own soul, but he who heeds rebuke gets understanding.
Prov. 15:32

## FAITH

The fear of man brings a snare, but whoever trusts in the LORD shall be safe.
Prov. 29:25

## FRIENDS

He who walks with wise men will be wise, but the companion of fools will be destroyed.
Prov. 13:20

## GOSSIP
Where there is no wood, the fire goes out; and
where there is no talebearer, strife ceases.
Prov. 26:20

## GUIDANCE
For the commandment is a lamp, and the law a
light; reproofs of instruction are the way of life.
Prov. 6:23

## HUMILITY
A prudent man foresees evil and hides himself;
the simple pass on and are punished.
Prov. 27:12

## KNOWLEDGE
The heart of the prudent acquires knowledge,
and the ear of the wise seeks knowledge.
Prov. 18:15

## LAZINESS
He who has a slack hand becomes poor, but
the hand of the diligent makes rich.
Prov. 10:4

## LOVE
Hatred stirs up strife, but love covers all sins.
Prov. 10:12

## MOTIVATION

Every way of a man is right in his own eyes,
but the LORD weighs the hearts.
Prov. 21:2

## PATIENCE

A faithful man will abound with blessings,
but he who hastens to be rich will
not go unpunished.
Prov. 28:20

## PEACE

When a man's ways please the LORD, he
makes even his enemies to be at peace
with him.
Prov. 16:7

## PERSISTENCE

Do you see a man who excels in his work? He
will stand before kings; he will not stand before
unknown men.
Prov. 22:29

## PRIDE

Pride goes before destruction, and a haughty
spirit before a fall.
Prov. 16:18

## RIGHTEOUSNESS
But the path of the just is like the shining sun,
that shines ever brighter unto the perfect day.
Prov. 4:18

## SIN
Evil pursues sinners, but to the righteous,
good shall be repaid.
Prov. 13:21

## TEMPTATION
Do not enter the path of the wicked, and do
not walk in the way of evil.
Prov. 4:14

## TRUST
Trust in the LORD with all your heart, and
lean not on your own understanding. In all
your ways acknowledge Him, and He shall
direct your paths.
Prov. 3:5-6

## VISION
Where there is no revelation, the people cast
off restraint; but happy is he who
keeps the law.
Prov. 29:18

## WISDOM

Wisdom is the principal thing; therefore get
wisdom. And in all your getting, get
understanding.

Prov. 4:7

## WORDS

A man has joy by the answer of his mouth, and
a word spoken in due season, how good it is!

Prov. 15:23

# ABOUT THE AUTHOR

John Mason is the founder and president of Insight International, an organization dedicated to helping people reach their dreams and fulfill their destiny. He is an ordained minister who speaks at numerous churches and conferences throughout the United States and abroad.

He has authored several best-selling books including:

**An Enemy Called Average**

**You're Born An Original—Don't Die A Copy!**

**Let Go of Whatever Makes You Stop**

**Conquering An Enemy Called Average**

**Know Your Limits—Then Ignore Them**

**Ask . . . (Life's Most Important Answers Are Found in Asking the Right Questions)**

You can contact him at :

**John Mason**
P.O. Box 54996
Tulsa, OK 74155

Prov. 29:25

The fear of man brings a snare,

but whoever trusts in

the Lord shall be safe.

## THE HARRISON HOUSE VISION

Proclaiming the truth and the power

Of the Gospel of Jesus Christ

With excellence;

Challenging Christians to

Live victoriously,

Grow spiritually,

Know God intimately